MW00814167

LIVING IN STYLE
MOUNTAIN CHALETS

Edited by Gisela Rich

Thanks to Susanne Lanz
for her expert advice

teNeues

CONTENTS

Introduction 4

Bärenhütte *Kitzbühel, Austria* 10

Rock House *Kitzbühel, Austria* 14

Haus Hild *Kitzbühel, Austria* 20

Alpine Mountain Retreat Kitzbühel *Kitzbühel, Austria* 24

Chalet in Kitzbühel *Kitzbühel, Austria* 28

Chalet Tauern *Kitzbühel, Austria* 32

Chalet Sonnenhof *Seefeld, Austria* 36

Stadl am Tunauberg *South Styria, Austria* 40

Amazon Creek *Chamonix, France* 44

Chalet Atlantique *Courchevel, France* 48

Ferme de Montagne *Les Gets, France* 54

Chalet Eco Farm *Les Houches, France* 58

Le Chalet des Fermes de Marie *Megève, France* 62

Le Chalet *Megève, France* 66

Chalet Les Brames *Méribel, France* 70

Chalet la Transhumance *Saint-Martin-de-Belleville, France* ... 74

House in Val d'Isère *Val d'Isère, France* 78

BergLodge *Nesselwang, Germany* 82

San Lorenzo Mountain Lodge *St. Lorenzen, Dolomites, Italy* ... 86

Mountain Lodge Trysil *Trøgstad, Norway* 90

The Villa at Copperhill Mountain Lodge *Åre, Sweden* 94

Chalet Rougemont *Gstaad Valley, Switzerland* 98

Chesa Farrer *Celerina, Switzerland* 102

Julierhof *Champfèr, Switzerland* 106

Chesa Alta *La Punt, Switzerland* 110

House in Les Collons *Les Collons, Switzerland* 114

Chesa Cresta *St. Moritz, Switzerland* 118

Chesa Musi *St. Moritz, Switzerland* 122

Chesa Nova *St. Moritz, Switzerland* 126

Chesa Pichalain *St. Moritz, Switzerland* 130

Der Turm *St. Moritz, Switzerland* 134

La Quinta *St. Moritz, Switzerland* 138

Olympiastadion *St. Moritz, Switzerland* 142

Residenzia Rosatsch *St. Moritz, Switzerland* 146

La Stailina *Suvretta, Switzerland* 150

Hidden Dragon *Valais, Switzerland* 156

Chalet in Verbier *Verbier, Switzerland* 160

The Lodge *Verbier, Switzerland* 164

Zermatt Peak *Zermatt, Switzerland* 168

Belmont *Whistler, British Columbia, Canada* 172

Bighorn *Revelstoke, British Columbia, Canada* 176

Pioneer Springs *Aspen, Colorado, USA* 180

Chalet Antonia *Aspen, Colorado, USA* 184

Mountain Star Residence *Avon, Colorado, USA* 188

Rosenbach Residence *Vail, Colorado, USA* 192

Urban Chalet *Park City, Utah, USA* 196

Miyabi and Tsubaki *Niseko, Japan* 202

Zekkei *Hirafu, Japan* 206

House at the Mountain *Karuizawa, Japan* 210

Whare Kea Lodge & Chalet *Wanaka, New Zealand* 214

Index 218

Credits & Imprint 220

Introduction

Like a house overlooking the ocean, an isolated cabin in the mountains is one of those places we dream about: It represents a life in harmony with nature, far from the pressures of everyday life. On our journey high into the mountains, we will introduce you to some of these extraordinary places: mountain chalets in idyllic locations as well as their interiors. It is impossible to look at these houses apart from their surroundings, because nature and the landscape give these structures their unique character. The intimate dialog between lifestyle and the dramatic mountains is what makes chalets such exciting dwellings.

Modern Alpine architecture is characterized by expansive walls of glass. It is the views in particular—whether of snowy landscapes or untouched nature—that allow these houses to connect to their surroundings. This book showcases chalets whose panoramas exhibit such a surreal beauty that they could have been painted by an artist. Also exhibiting a direct relationship to their environment, the interiors of these chalets frequently draw upon regional materials, including animal skins, loden fabric, leather, natural stone, and solid wood. At these high altitudes, you are just as likely to find luxury, wellness, and design elements familiar from upscale residences as you are the more traditional styles.

This book features gorgeous chalets from around the world. Many are located in famous ski resorts, while others are more secluded. In their individual ways, they offer new, unusual, and surprising home design ideas. Some structures have a history dating back to the 16th century; their current owners are committed to continuing traditional Alpine architecture. Some of these rustic chalets appear to have been lifted straight out of a fairy tale, while others bear witness to the fact that contemporary architecture and design have long since conquered even the highest elevations.

Despite the international orientation of this book with chalets in Europe, the United States, Japan, and New Zealand, it does have one special focus: St. Moritz. This village in Switzerland is arguably the most famous ski resort in the world and offers a concentration of elegant mountain chalets unlike anywhere else in the world. As a cosmopolitan Alpine village, St. Moritz is a microcosm that stylistically represents the entire range of contemporary living in high-altitude regions. For the first time ever, this book offers glimpses of interiors that have never before been seen publicly.

No matter where they are located, exclusive chalets are the stuff dreams are made of. There is one thing all these places have in common: Their owners use them differently than an apartment in the city. People retreat to the mountains to find time for themselves and to renew their ties to nature outside of the hectic pace of everyday life. Because these chalets are used as vacation homes or retreats, they provide a palette for design that gives free reign to fantasy and unconventional ideas. Discovering and exploring this extraordinary world is both inspiring and surprising.

Einleitung

Die einsame Hütte in den Bergen gehört wie das Haus am Meer zu unseren Sehnsuchtsorten. Wir verbinden damit ein Leben in und mit der Natur, abseits der Lasten und Nöte des Alltags. Auf unserer Reise hoch hinauf in die Berge stellen wir Ihnen einige dieser außergewöhnlichen Orte vor: Bergchalets in idyllischer Lage sowie deren Interieurs. Die Häuser sind nie losgelöst von ihrer Umgebung zu betrachten, denn die Natur und die Landschaft verleihen den Gebäuden einen einzigartigen Charakter. Es ist dieser intensive Dialog zwischen dem Wohnen und der dramatischen Bergwelt, der das Chalet zu einer so spannenden Hauskategorie macht.

Die übergroßen, voll verglasten Fensterfronten sind heute das charakteristische Merkmal des alpinen Bauens. Vor allem die Ausblicke – hinein in verträumte Schneelandschaften oder in die wilde Natur – lassen die Häuser in Verbindung treten mit ihrer Umgebung. Dieser Band zeigt Chalets, deren Panoramen so unwirklich schön wirken, als seien sie von einem Künstler gemalt. Auch die Inneneinrichtung steht bei der Berghütte in direkter Beziehung zum Umfeld. Es sind immer wieder Materialien regionalen Ursprungs verwendet, zum Beispiel Tierfelle, Loden, Leder, Naturstein und Massivholz. Neben den traditionellen Stilen finden sich in der Höhe aber ebenso Luxus, Wellness und Design, wie wir es vom gehobenen Wohnen her kennen.

Die traumhaften Chalets aus diesem Buch sind über die ganze Welt verteilt. Viele davon befinden sich in berühmten Wintersportorten, einige suchen die Abgeschiedenheit. Jedes Haus überrascht auf seine individuelle Weise mit neuen, außergewöhnlichen Wohnideen. Manche Gebäude blicken auf eine Geschichte, die bis ins 16. Jahrhundert zurückreicht. Deren jetzige Inhaber kümmern sich engagiert um die Fortführung der alpinen Bautraditionen. Ebenso öffnen sich die Türen zu urigen Hütten im rustikalen Stil, die aussehen, als seien sie einer Märchenwelt entsprungen. Andere Beispiele zeigen, dass auch die zeitgenössische Architektur und der Designkult die Höhenlagen längst erobert haben.

Trotz der internationalen Ausrichtung dieses Buches mit Chalets in Europa, den USA, Japan und Neuseeland gibt es einen Schwerpunkt: St. Moritz, der wohl berühmteste Wintersportort der Welt, bietet weltweit eine einzigartige Dichte an eleganten Bergchalets. Die kosmopolitische Alpenstadt stellt einen Mikrokosmos dar, der stilistisch die ganze Bandbreite des gegenwärtigen Wohnens in der Höhe abbildet. Erstmalig sind hier Einblicke in Interieurs gewährt, die zuvor öffentlich nicht zu sehen waren.

Überall auf der Welt finden sich exklusive Chalets, die zum Träumen einladen. Was alle Häuser gemein haben: Ihre Inhaber nutzen sie anders als die Wohnung in der Stadt. Die Menschen ziehen sich in die Berge zurück, um dort jenseits der alltäglichen Hektik mit sich und der Natur zu sein. Wegen der Nutzung als Ferienwohnung oder Rückzugsort erlaubt das Chalet eine Gestaltung, die mehr Phantasie und viele unkonventionelle Ideen zulässt. Diese außergewöhnliche Welt zu entdecken, ist deshalb überraschend und inspirierend zugleich.

Introduction

Le chalet perdu dans la montagne et la villa au bord de la mer ont en commun l'émotion que suscite leur simple évocation. Ils évoquent l'harmonie avec la nature, loin des tracas du quotidien. Sur la route qui va nous mener à travers les massifs montagneux de la planète, nous allons vous présenter des endroits extraordinaires : des chalets édifiés sur des sites idylliques, mis en valeur par des intérieurs tout aussi splendides. Le bâti ne peut être dissocié de l'environnement, car la nature et le paysage lui confèrent son caractère unique. Cette relation intense entre la fonction de l'habitat et le spectacle de la montagne place les chalets dans une catégorie de logement absolument passionnante.

Le recours aux baies vitrées surdimensionnées sur l'ensemble de la façade est devenu caractéristique de la construction en montagne, son intégration dans l'environnement dépendant avant tout de la vue dont elle dispose — que ce soit sur la neige de paysages de rêve ou sur une nature sauvage et préservée. Les panoramas qu'offrent les chalets présentés dans ce livre semblent avoir été peints sur une toile, tellement leur beauté paraît irréelle. La décoration intérieure des chalets est, elle aussi, indissociable de l'environnement. Si l'on y retrouve toujours des matériaux locaux comme la peau, le loden, le cuir, la pierre naturelle ou le bois massif, ces maisons d'altitude réservent également une place privilégiée au luxe, au bien-être et au design, conformément aux attentes dans un logement haut de gamme.

Les merveilles réunies dans ce livre se trouvent dans le monde entier. Bon nombre de ces chalets se situent dans de célèbres stations de sports d'hiver, tandis que d'autres témoignent d'une recherche d'isolement. Chaque maison est surprenante à sa manière, grâce à des idées novatrices ou hors du commun. L'histoire de certains de ces bâtiments remonte au XVIᵉ siècle. Leurs propriétaires actuels manifestent un réel engagement à faire perdurer les traditions constructives montagnardes. Parfois, le chalet présenté ouvre ses portes sur un intérieur d'apparence rustique, semblant directement tiré de l'univers d'un conteur. D'autres exemples prouvent que l'architecture contemporaine et le culte du design ont gagné depuis longtemps les cimes de nos montagnes.

S'il est vrai que ce livre contient des exemples de chalets situés en Europe, aux États-Unis, au Japon et en Nouvelle-Zélande, il met néanmoins l'accent sur celle qui est sans doute la ville de sports d'hiver la plus célèbre au monde et qui présente une concentration exceptionnelle de chalets cossus : Saint-Moritz. Cette ville alpine très cosmopolite reprend, d'un point de vue stylistique, toute la palette de l'habitat contemporain en altitude. Pour la première fois, il est possible de découvrir des intérieurs qui, jusqu'à présent, étaient totalement inconnus du public.

Quelle que soit la région du monde où se dressent ces authentiques invitations au rêve, les chalets de luxe ont un point commun : leurs propriétaires n'en font certainement pas la même utilisation qu'un appartement en ville. D'une manière générale, les hommes se retirent dans la montagne pour s'éloigner du tumulte de la vie quotidienne et se rapprocher de la nature, mais aussi pour se ressourcer. En sa qualité de résidence de vacances ou de retraite, le chalet autorise plus de fantaisie et permet de laisser libre cours aux idées les plus originales. La découverte de ce monde extraordinaire se révèle être pleine de surprises et source d'inspiration.

Bärenhütte

Kitzbühel, Austria

Located in the Kitzbühel Alps, the Bärenhütte was renovated and refurnished by the current owners in 2005. They made the conscious decision not to use the typical Alpine style for the interior spaces. Walls constructed of wide wooden planks and massive ceiling beams give it the feel of a log cabin from Canada or the United States. Fabrics in colorful Indian patterns reinforce this impression. Bears in the form of figures or images appear as a recurrent motif throughout the decor. Numerous animal hides combined with the magnificent elk head mounted above the fireplace give guests the impression that it is no Alpine farmer who lives here, but rather a trapper ready to head out hunting. A specially designed kitchen is truly unique: All of the cabinets are completely clad in birch bark.

Die Bärenhütte in den Kitzbüheler Alpen haben die jetzigen Besitzer im Jahr 2005 umgebaut und neu eingerichtet. Die Innenräume sind bewusst nicht im typisch alpenländischen Stil gestaltet. Wände aus breiten Holzbohlen und wuchtiges Dachgebälk erinnern eher an eine Blockhütte in den Wäldern Kanadas oder der USA. Die vielen Textilien mit den farbenfrohen, indianischen Mustern verstärken diesen Eindruck. Bei der Dekoration taucht immer wieder in Form von Figuren oder Bildern das Bärenmotiv auf. Auch die vielen Tierfelle sowie der prachtvolle Elchkopf über dem Kamin lassen vermuten, dass hier kein Alpenbauer sondern ein Trapper auf der Jagd zu Hause ist. Die eigens angefertigte Küche ist ein Unikat der ganz besonderen Art: Alle Schränke sind komplett mit Birkenrinde verkleidet.

En 2005, le « chalet des ours » situé dans les environs de Kitzbühel, a été transformé par ses propriétaires actuels, qui ont choisi de redécorer l'intérieur dans un style volontairement atypique pour la région. En effet, l'imposante charpente et les larges planches de bois qui recouvrent les murs, associées à de nombreux tissus aux motifs indiens colorés, font penser à une cabane en rondins au cœur d'une forêt nord-américaine. Il est vrai aussi que les nombreuses peaux, tout comme la splendide tête d'élan qui domine la cheminée, évoquent plus la maison d'un trappeur que celle d'un éleveur des alpages. Le thème des ours est également repris dans de nombreux éléments décoratifs, tels que les figurines et tableaux. Par ailleurs, la finition de la cuisine est absolument unique : tous les placards sont entièrement habillés d'écorce de bouleau.

Even the bathroom with its antique fittings and the cozily furnished bedroom feel like scenery from a Jack London adventure novel.

Auch das Bad mit seinen antiken Armaturen sowie das gemütlich möblierte Schlafzimmer erinnern an eine Szenerie aus einem Abenteuerroman von Jack London.

La salle de bain et sa robinetterie ancienne, ainsi que la chambre et ses meubles absolument charmants évoquent les scènes d'un roman d'aventures de Jack London.

Rock House

Kitzbühel, Austria

Susanne Lanz moved to Kitzbühel twelve years ago and discovered her passion for Tyrolean architecture. As a project developer, she has selected the furnishings and had a hand in the development of numerous buildings in the region. Susanne Lanz and her family live in the Rock House. With its large front glass façade and open layout, the building could also be located in California—if it weren't for the myriad details and the use of materials which clearly connect it to the region. Susanne Lanz works whenever possible with antique wood as well as with materials such as animal furs, iron, loden fabric, and natural stone. She combines these regional design elements with contemporary design and art, an approach that enables her to create a modern interpretation of the Alpine architectural tradition.

Vor zwölf Jahren ist Susanne Lanz nach Kitzbühel gekommen und hat dort ihre Leidenschaft für die Tiroler Baukunst entdeckt. Als Bauträgerin hat sie zahlreiche Gebäude in der Region ausgestattet und entwickelt. Das Rock House bewohnt Susanne Lanz zusammen mit ihrer Familie selbst. Mit seinen großen Glasfronten und den offenen Grundrissen könnte das Gebäude auch in Kalifornien stehen – wären da nicht die vielen Details und die verwendeten Materialien, die einen deutlichen Bezug zur Region herstellen. Susanne Lanz arbeitet, wann immer es möglich ist, mit Altholz, ebenso mit Materialien wie Eisen, Loden, Tierfellen oder Naturstein. Sie kombiniert diese regionalen Gestaltungselemente mit zeitgenössischem Design und Gegenwartskunst. Auf diese Weise gelingt ihr eine moderne Interpretation der alpinen Bautradition.

Quand Susanne Lanz s'est rendue à Kitzbühel il y a douze ans, elle y a développé une véritable passion pour l'architecture tyrolienne. En tant que promotrice, elle a participé à l'aménagement de nombreux bâtiments de la région avant de s'installer avec sa famille dans le chalet Rock House. Avec sa large façade vitrée, ce bâtiment aux espaces ouverts pourrait tout aussi bien se situer en Californie – s'il n'existait pas tant de références à la région de Kitzbühel, que ce soit dans les matériaux utilisés ou dans d'autres détails. Susanne Lanz aime travailler dans la mesure du possible avec du bois ancien, mais aussi avec des matériaux comme l'acier, le loden, la peau et la pierre naturelle. Elle intègre ces éléments décoratifs traditionnels dans un style moderne et des œuvres d'art contemporain, réinterprétant ainsi la construction alpine traditionnelle.

Suffused with light, the Rock House feels as elegant as a structure by California architect Richard Neutra, yet it offers the warmth and comfort of a Tyrolean Holzstube, or wooden room.

Das lichtdurchflutete Rock House wirkt so elegant wie ein Bau des kalifornischen Architekten Richard Neutra, bietet aber ebenso die Wärme und Behaglichkeit einer Tiroler Holzstube.

Baignée de soleil, cette Rock House rivalise d'élégance avec les constructions de l'architecte californien Richard Neutra, tout en proposant la chaleur et le bien-être d'une « stube » tyrolienne en bois.

Haus Hild

Kitzbühel, Austria

Haus Hild is a mountain chalet located on a property in the Tyrolean Alps that is just under an acre. The building's architecture blends a ground floor with plastered brick walls with a timber construction on the upper story. The wrap-around balconies are a typical feature of the region's architectural style. Inside, the house offers just over 6,800 square feet of living space and can accommodate guests in five bedrooms with attached private bathrooms. The living room features an impressive ceiling height of just over 16 feet, which is unusual for a chalet. Amenities also include a swimming pool, sauna, and fitness room. Wood dominates the furnishings. The shapes are plain and are reminiscent of the simple style of a farmer's cottage. Modern furniture and decor blend harmoniously with the furnishings.

Die Berghütte Haus Hild steht auf einem Grundstück von 3 800 Quadratmetern in den Tiroler Alpen. Die Architektur des Gebäudes kombiniert ein gemauertes Untergeschoss mit einem Obergeschoss in Holzbauweise. Die umlaufenden Balkons sind typisch für die Bautradition der Region. Im Inneren verfügt das Anwesen über eine Wohn- und Nutzfläche von insgesamt 640 Quadratmetern. Die Bewohner finden Platz in fünf Schlafzimmern mit angegliederten Bädern. Im Wohnzimmer beeindruckt die für eine Hütte außergewöhnliche Deckenhöhe von fünf Metern. Zur Ausstattung gehören weiterhin Schwimmbad, Sauna und Fitnessraum. Bei der Einrichtung ist Holz das dominierende Material. Die Formen sind schlicht und erinnern an den einfachen Stil einer Bauernhütte. Modern gestalte Möbel und Dekors fügen sich harmonisch in die Einrichtung ein.

Le chalet Haus Hild est construit sur un terrain de 3 800 mètres carrés au cœur des Alpes tyroliennes. L'architecture du bâtiment associe un rez-de-chaussée maçonné et un étage à ossature bois. Les balcons qui entourent la maison sont typiques des méthodes de construction de la région. À l'intérieur, la demeure offre au total 640 mètres carrés de surface habitable. Les occupants disposent de cinq chambres à coucher avec salles de bain attenantes. Dans le salon, les cinq mètres de hauteur de plafond sont étonnants pour un chalet. En matière de décoration, le bois constitue le matériau le plus utilisé. Les formes sont simples et rappellent la sobriété d'une ferme de montagne tandis que les meubles et autres attributs modernes sont harmonieusement intégrés. Enfin, le chalet est équipé d'une piscine, d'un sauna et d'une salle de sport.

The turned banisters, animal furs, and hunting trophies are typical elements of the Alpine style. The bathrooms, on the other hand, feature modern design.

Das gedrechselte Treppengeländer, die Tierfelle und die Jagdtrophäen sind typisch alpine Stilelemente. Bei der Sanitärtechnik im Bad findet man aber auch modernes Design.

Les montants torsadés de la rampe, les peaux et les trophées de chasse sont autant d'éléments décoratifs typiquement alpins. La salle de bain dispose d'un équipement moderne.

Alpine Mountain Retreat Kitzbühel

Kitzbühel, Austria

The Alpine Mountain Retreat in the Kitzbühel Alps was built in the 1960s. The current owners acquired the house and converted it in 2003–04. The cheery furnishings are well thought out and were designed by the owners with great attention to detail. The style combines Alpine coziness with metropolitan elegance. Pale-colored coniferous wood so typical for the region dominates the walls, ceilings, and floors. Warm woods are also used in the furniture and the doors of the kitchen cabinets. While designing the interior spaces, the owners chose to use vivid reds and patterned fabrics to contrast with the wood. Carefully selected antique objects and historic paintings on the walls complete the ambience of upscale living.

Das Alpine Mountain Retreat in den Kitzbüheler Alpen wurde in den 60er Jahren erbaut. In den Jahren 2003/04 haben die jetzigen Besitzer das Haus erworben und umgebaut. Die freundliche Einrichtung wirkt durchdacht und wurde von den Eigentümern mit viel Liebe zum Detail gestaltet. Der Stil verbindet alpenländische Gemütlichkeit mit großstädtischer Eleganz. An den Wänden, Decken und Böden dominieren helle Nadelhölzer, wie sie für die Region typisch sind. Auch bei den Möbeln und Küchenfronten ist Holz in warmen Tönen verwendet. Als Kontrast dazu arbeiteten die Besitzer bei der Gestaltung der Innenräume mit kräftigem Rot sowie gemusterten Textilien. Die sorgfältig ausgewählten antiken Deko-Objekte sowie die historischen Gemälde an den Wänden vervollständigen das Ambiente einer gehobenen Wohnkultur.

L'Alpine Mountain Retreat, situé dans les environs de Kitzbühel dans les Alpes, a été érigé dans les années 60. Les propriétaires actuels en ont fait l'acquisition en 2003, puis l'ont transformé jusqu'en 2004. L'aménagement a été mûrement réfléchi et démontre un amour du détail. Le style réunit l'ambiance chaleureuse du chalet alpin et l'élégance des métropoles. Sur les murs, les plafonds et les sols, c'est le bois clair des résineux typiques de la région qui domine. De même, les propriétaires ont principalement choisi des tons chauds pour le bois des meubles, ainsi que des portes de placards de la cuisine. En matière d'aménagement intérieur, ils ont joué sur des rouges intenses ainsi que sur des tissus à motifs pour contraster avec le bois. La sélection rigoureuse d'objets anciens et les tableaux à caractère historique témoignent d'un art de vivre raffiné.

Chalet in Kitzbühel

Kitzbühel, Austria

Located on a generous half acre, this luxurious 9,400-square-foot chalet is surrounded by expansive and secluded parkland. The interior reflects the traditional Tyrolean style. The exposed beams in particular reflect the typical Alpine construction. Living spaces occupy different levels and spill out onto a spacious outdoor terrace. The living room with its gallery is the architectural highlight of the chalet. Through the huge panoramic windows, guests can enjoy magnificent views of the Hahnenkamm and the Wilder Kaiser mountain ranges. The wellness area is equipped with a 36 x 13 foot indoor pool, sauna, steam bath, relaxation room, and fitness studio. Thanks to its Alpine panorama, the pool feels like a fresh, clear Alpine lake.

Das luxuriöse Chalet befindet sich auf einem 2 384 Quadratmeter großen Grundstück und verfügt über insgesamt 876 Quadratmeter Wohn- und Nutzfläche. Das Gebäude ist umgeben von einer weitläufigen, nicht einsehbaren Parkanlage. Die Inneneinrichtung orientiert sich am traditionellen Tiroler Stil. Vor allem die freigelegte Balkenkonstruktion verweist auf die typisch alpine Bauweise. Das Wohnen findet auf unterschiedlichen Ebenen sowie der großflächigen Außenterrasse statt. Architektonischer Höhepunkt ist das Wohnzimmer mit seiner Galerie. Durch die riesigen Panoramafenster hat der Bewohner einen traumhaften Blick auf die Gebirgszüge des Hahnenkamms und des Wilden Kaisers. Der Wellnessbereich ist ausgestattet mit einem 11 x 4 Meter großen Hallenbad, Sauna, Dampfbad, Ruheraum und Fitness-studio. Der Pool wirkt durch sein Alpenpanorama wie ein frischer, klarer Bergsee.

Le luxueux chalet se trouve sur un domaine de 2 384 mètres carrés et compte plus de 876 mètres carrés de surface habitable. Le bâtiment est niché dans un vaste parc qui l'abrite parfaitement des regards. La décoration intérieure suit les codes du style tyrolien traditionnel. On retrouve notamment les poutres apparentes typiques des constructions alpines. Ici, les lieux de vie sont répartis entre les différents niveaux du chalet, sans oublier son immense terrasse. Avec sa galerie, la salle de séjour constitue une véritable merveille architectonique. Les gigantesques fenêtres panoramiques offrent aux occupants des lieux une vue splendide sur la chaîne du Hahnenkamm et du Wilder Kaiser. L'espace bien-être est équipé d'une piscine de 11 x 4 mètres, d'un sauna, d'un hammam et d'une salle de sport. Le panorama alpin de la piscine procure la sensation de fraîcheur des eaux cristallines d'un lac de montagne.

*The staircase leads up into the livingroom gallery. Floors are made of natural stone
and feature the occasional animal hide as rugs, just like in a hunting lodge.*

*Die Treppe führt hinauf in die Wohnzimmergalerie. Die Böden sind
aus Naturstein und wie in einer Jagdhütte mit Tierfellen ausgelegt.*

*L'escalier mène à la galerie du séjour. Les sols en pierre naturelle
sont décorés de peaux comme dans une cabane de chasseurs.*

Chalet Tauern

Kitzbühel, Austria

Chalet Tauern is located on the sunny side of Kitzbühel. From the cozy living room sofa, guests can enjoy unimpeded views of Hahnenkamm Mountain and the Streif, one of the most dreaded and dangerous ski race courses in the world. The 5,600-square-foot chalet features furnishings tailored to contemporary living. Two of the four bedrooms as well as the master suite occupy the lower level. Every bedroom includes its own private bathroom. Susanne Lanz placed the living area with the kitchen and two dining spaces on the upper level. In addition, the chalet features its own spa. A 46-foot pool with a counter-current system, a Turkish steam bath, and a large relaxation area with a flat-screen TV offer many luxurious ways to unwind.

Auf der Sonnenseite Kitzbühels befindet sich das Chalet Tauern. Vom gemütlichen Wohnzimmersofa geht der Blick direkt auf den Hahnenkamm und die Streif, eine der gefürchtetsten und gefährlichsten Skirennstrecken der Welt. Das Chalet bietet den Bewohnern auf einer Fläche von 520 Quadratmetern eine Ausstattung, die auf zeitgemäße Wohnbedürfnisse zugeschnitten ist. Im unteren Stockwerk befinden sich zwei der insgesamt vier Schlafzimmer sowie die Mastersuite. Alle Schlafzimmer sind mit Ensuite-Bädern ausgestattet. Im oberen Stockwerk hat Susanne Lanz den Wohnbereich mit der Küche und zwei unterschiedlichen Essplätzen untergebracht. Das Chalet verfügt weiterhin über ein hauseigenes Spa. Ein 14 Meter langer Pool mit Gegenstromanlage, ein türkisches Dampfbad sowie eine großzügige Relaxzone mit TV-Monitor sorgen für luxuriöse Entspannung.

Le Chalet Tauern se situe sur les versants ensoleillés de Kitzbühel. Assis sur le moelleux canapé du séjour, le visiteur peut contempler le Hahnenkamm et la Streif, une des pistes de descente les plus redoutables au monde. Le chalet offre à ses occupants une surface de 520 mètres carrés, aménagée sur mesure pour correspondre aux tendances actuelles en matière de style de vie. Au niveau inférieur se trouvent deux des quatre chambres à coucher ainsi que la suite de maître. Toutes les chambres à coucher disposent d'une salle de bain. À l'étage, Susanne Lanz a mis en place le séjour comptant une cuisine et deux salles à manger. Dans le spa du chalet, détente rime avec luxe, grâce à une piscine de 14 mètres avec turbine de nage à contre-courant, un hammam turc, ainsi qu'une vaste zone de relaxation avec un écran de télévision.

The bioethanol fireplace in the master suite wraps around the corner, a unique design feature. Seated at the large table, guests can enjoy Tyrolean cuisine along with spectacular views of the Kitzbühel Alps.

Der Bioethanol-Kamin in der Mastersuite ist auf ungewöhnliche Weise über Eck gebaut. An der großen Tafel genießen die Bewohner die Tiroler Küche und den spektakulären Blick auf die Kitzbüheler Alpen.

Originalité de la suite de maître : sa cheminée d'angle au bioéthanol. Sur la grande table, les occupants se délectent autant la cuisine tyrolienne que de la vue spectaculaire sur les montagnes de Kitzbühel.

Chalet Sonnenhof

Seefeld, Austria

Chalet Sonnenhof is located right next to a little forest. Guests wouldn't guess that the center of the small Alpine town is nearby. The chalet is located in the midst of extensive farmland and can only be reached via a private lane. The façade of the house has retained its traditional Tyrolean chalet style. Large panoramic windows offer a view of the Alpine landscape. The floor plan and the roof beams have an open design that gives the structure a modern loft character. The furniture was made by designers from Italy, France, and South Africa. In addition, Susanne Lanz uses many local materials, such as loden cloth, fur, oak, and spruce. The kitchen features high-quality technology from Gaggenau.

In direkter Nachbarschaft zu einem kleinen Wäldchen befindet sich das Chalet Sonnenhof. Vom nahen Zentrum des Alpenstädtchens spürt man hier nichts mehr. Das Gebäude liegt inmitten weitläufiger Ackerflächen, nur zu erreichen über einen privaten Weg. Die Hausfassade ist im klassischen Tiroler Hüttenstil gehalten. Großzügige Fensterfronten geben den Blick frei auf die Alpenlandschaft. Die Grundrisse sowie die Balkenkonstruktion im Dachbereich hat der Architekt offen gestaltet, wodurch das Gebäude einen modernen Loftcharakter erhält. Die Möbel stammen von Designern aus Italien, Frankreich und Südafrika. Daneben verwendet Susanne Lanz viele heimische Materialien, wie Loden, Pelz oder Eichen- und Fichtenholz. In der Küche findet sich hochwertige Technik von Gaggenau.

Le Chalet Sonnenhof se trouve à deux pas d'un petit bois. Malgré la proximité du centre-ville, il est impossible de percevoir quoi que ce soit de la charmante bourgade alpine. Le bâtiment situé au milieu de vastes champs est accessible uniquement par un chemin privé. La façade arbore un style tyrolien classique. De généreuses baies vitrées cadrent le paysage alpin. L'architecte a opté pour un plan libre et une charpente apparente afin de donner au bâtiment le caractère moderne d'un loft. Les meubles sont de designers italiens, français et sud-africains. Par ailleurs, Susanne Lanz a fait appel à des matériaux locaux comme le loden, la peau, le chêne et l'épicéa. L'électroménager haut de gamme de la cuisine est signé Gaggenau.

The spa and bathrooms have a puristic design. The upper living area is comfortable and offers a fantastic view of the Alps.

Spa und Bäder sind puristisch gestaltet. Der obere Wohnbereich bietet viel Komfort und einen traumhaften Ausblick auf die Alpen.

L'aménagement du spa et des salles de bain est très épuré. L'étage offre un grand confort ainsi qu'une vue merveilleuse sur les Alpes.

Stadl am Tunauberg

South Styria, Austria

Stadl am Tunauberg is one of the high-class vacation houses of the company PURESLeben (which means "pure life"), located in the Austrian region of Southern Styria. The architects retained the original barn character of the building by leaving the gable roof and its wooden beams exposed after the renovations. The barn has a total of 800 square feet on two levels. The living area includes an open, modern kitchen with a fireplace. In the bedroom on the upper level, guests feel like they are in a hayloft. The large windows offer an unimpeded view of the vineyards and the gentle rolling hills of South Styria. In close collaboration with the Neue Wiener Werkstätte, the interior decor combines modern design with regional style elements. After a visit to the sauna, a natural pond in the garden offers a lovely place to cool off.

Der Stadl am Tunauberg gehört zu den Premium-Ferienhäusern des Unternehmens PURESLeben in der südlichen Steiermark. Den ursprünglichen Stadlcharakter des Gebäudes haben die Architekten erhalten. Das Giebeldach sowie dessen Holzgebälk bleiben deshalb auch nach den Umbauten weiterhin sichtbar. Der Stadl verfügt über insgesamt 75 Quadratmeter Wohnfläche auf zwei Ebenen. Zum Wohnbereich gehört eine moderne offene Küche mit Kamin. Im Schlafzimmer des oberen Stockwerks fühlt sich der Bewohner wie auf einem Heuboden. Die Fensterfronten geben den Blick frei auf die Weinberge und die sanften Hügel der Südsteiermark. Die Inneneinrichtung kombiniert in enger Zusammenarbeit mit der Neuen Wiener Werkstätte moderne Designsprache mit regionalen Stilelementen. Nach dem Saunabesuch bietet ein Naturteich im Garten Abkühlung.

La maison Stadl am Tunauberg fait partie des maisons de vacances supérieures gerées par la société PURESLeben (soit « la vie pure ») en Styrie du Sud. Les architectes ont su préserver le caractère original de la grange, ce qui explique la présence d'un toit à pignons ainsi que d'une charpente en bois laissée apparente après les transformations. La Stadl dispose d'un total de 75 mètres carrés de surface habitable répartie sur deux niveaux. Intégrée à la partie séjour, une cuisine ouverte et moderne jouxte la cheminée. Dans la chambre de l'étage, les occupants se sentent comme dans un grenier à foin. Les baies vitrées donnent directement sur les vignobles vallonnés et les douces collines de la Styrie du Sud. La décoration intérieure associe un code de design contemporain à des éléments stylistiques régionaux grâce à la collaboration de la Neue Wiener Werkstätte. Le bassin naturel du jardin permet de se rafraîchir après un passage au sauna.

Amazon Creek

Chamonix, France

Amazon Creek is one of the most luxurious chalets in the French Mont Blanc valley and can accommodate ten guests in a total of five bedrooms. The facilities at Amazon Creek are equivalent to those of a top-rated hotel; the guest rooms include plasma TVs and iPod docking stations by Bose. The vacation home additionally features an outdoor pool, garden, and even its own home theater. The chalet's spa is equipped with a sauna, Turkish steam bath, and Jacuzzi. The furnishings in the chalet reference the typical Alpine style. Over the years, the wooden beams have taken on a dark patina and their age is reflected in the fissures and knotholes in the wood. The hunting trophies and the deer antlers fashioned into a chandelier are reminiscent of a classic mountain lodge.

Amazon Creek gehört zu den luxuriösesten Chalets im französischen Mont-Blanc-Tal. Zehn Personen können in insgesamt fünf Schlafzimmern übernachten. Die Ausstattung von Amazon Creek ist vergleichbar mit der eines hochklassigen Hotels. So finden die Gäste zum Beispiel auf ihren Zimmern Plasma-TV-Geräte und iPod-Docking-Stationen von Bose. Das Ferienhaus verfügt zusätzlich über einen Freiluftpool, Garten und sogar ein eigenes Kino. Das hauseigene Spa ist ausgestattet mit Sauna, türkischem Dampfbad und Jacuzzi. Die Einrichtung setzt ganz auf den alpenländischen Stil. Die Holzbalken haben im Lauf der Jahre bereits eine dunkle Farbe angenommen und tragen in Form von Rissen und Astlöchern die Zeichen der Zeit. An eine klassische Berghütte erinnern die Jagdtrophäen und die zum Kronleuchter umfunktionierten Hirschgeweihe.

L'Amazon Creek compte parmi les plus luxueux chalets de la vallée de Chamonix. Ses cinq chambres peuvent héberger dix personnes. L'équipement de l'Amazon Creek est semblable à celui d'un hôtel de luxe. Dans leur chambre, les clients disposent par exemple d'un écran plasma et d'un amplificateur Bose avec dock iPod. En plus d'une piscine en plein air, cette résidence secondaire dispose d'un jardin et même d'une salle de cinéma. Le spa de la maison est équipé d'un sauna, d'un hammam turc et d'un jacuzzi. La décoration est entièrement réalisée dans un style montagnard. Au fil des années, le temps a patiné le bois de la charpente, dessinant quelques fissures entre les nœuds qui se dessèchent. Les trophées de chasse et les bois de cerfs transformés en lustre rappellent les chalets de montagne traditionnels.

Chalet Atlantique

Courchevel, France

The region surrounding the resort of Courchevel in the Savoy Alps is one of the most exclusive ski areas in Europe. With the Chalet Atlantique, London project management and design house Earlcrown has successfully built an ambitious luxury project in this extraordinary location. The chalet offers 4,360 square feet of space spread out over four levels. French interior designer Noëlle Bonnemaison, who designed the interiors for hotels in Saint-Tropez and Courchevel, also handled the interior design for this project. In her interiors, Bonnemaison mixes custom-made pieces with designer furniture. In her choice of materials, she displays a preference for furs, leather, and velour. The heavy beams, the fine wooden paneling on the walls, and the extravagant chandeliers turn the chalet into a unique place of tasteful luxury.

Die Region rund um den Ort Courchevel in den Savoyer Alpen gehört zu den exklusivsten Skigebieten Europas. Das Londoner Design- und Projektmanagementbüro Earlcrown hat an diesem außergewöhnlichen Ort mit dem Chalet Atlantique ein ambitioniertes Luxusprojekt realisiert. Das Chalet verfügt über 405 Quadratmeter Wohnfläche, verteilt auf vier Ebenen. Verantwortlich für die Inneneinrichtung ist die französische Interior-Designerin Noëlle Bonnemaison, die bereits Hotels in Saint-Tropez und Courchevel ausgestattet hat. Bonnemaison mischt für ihre Interieurs maßgefertigte Einrichtungsstücke mit Designermöbeln. Bei den Materialien zeigt sie eine Vorliebe für Pelz, Leder und Velours. Das schwere Gebälk, die edle Holzverkleidung an den Wänden sowie die extravaganten Leuchten machen das Chalet zu einem einzigartigen Ort des gediegenen Luxus.

Courchevel, en Savoie, compte parmi les stations de sports d'hiver les plus sélect d'Europe. C'est dans ce lieu hors du commun que le bureau de design et de maîtrise d'œuvre londonien Earlcrown a réalisé un projet d'habitation luxueuse : le Chalet Atlantique. Ce dernier dispose de plus de 405 mètres carrés de surface habitable répartie sur quatre niveaux. La décoration a été confiée à l'architecte d'intérieur française Noëlle Bonnemaison qui, par le passé, avait travaillé sur des projets d'hôtels à Courchevel et Saint-Tropez. Dans ses aménagements, Bonnemaison aime associer des éléments décoratifs créés sur mesure à des meubles design. Les peaux, le cuir et le velours sont ses matériaux de prédilection. L'imposante charpente, les élégantes boiseries sur les murs, ainsi que l'extravagance des luminaires font de ce chalet un lieu unique au luxe authentique.

Ferme de Montagne

Les Gets, France

This 350-year-old farmhouse is located in the Savoy Alps above the village of Les Gets, just an hour from Geneva. When the current owners discovered the building ten years ago, only the walls and wooden framing were still standing. During the renovations, they were able to completely retain the oak beams dating back to 1650. The old floors with stones from Burgundy, the entrance portal, and the windows are still in their original state as well. Today, the house offers the comforts of a five-star hotel while not losing any of its original charm. Heavy leather armchairs, wrought iron radiators, and ancient oak create an atmosphere that feels both rustic and comfortable. The style bears witness to a steadfast faith in what is real and genuine.

Das 350 Jahre alte Bauernhaus befindet sich in den Savoyer Alpen, oberhalb des Dorfes Les Gets, nur eine Stunde entfernt von Genf. Als die jetzigen Besitzer das Gebäude vor zehn Jahren entdeckt haben, standen nur noch das Gemäuer und die Holzkonstruktion. Bei der Renovierung haben sie das Eichenholz-Gebälk aus dem Jahr 1650 komplett erhalten. Ebenso sind die alten Böden mit Steinen aus dem Burgund, das Eingangsportal und die Fenster noch im Originalzustand. Das Haus bietet heute den Komfort eines Fünf-Sterne-Hotels, verliert dabei aber nichts von seinem ursprünglichen Charme. Die schweren Ledersessel, schmiedeeiserne Heizkörper und das uralte Eichenholz schaffen eine Atmosphäre, die sehr urig und gemütlich wirkt. Der Stil zeugt von einem unverrückbaren Glauben an das Echte und Unverfälschte.

Cette ancienne ferme a été construite au milieu du XVIIᵉ siècle sur les hauteurs des Gets, village savoyard situé à une heure de Genève. Lorsque les propriétaires actuels ont découvert le bâtiment il y a dix ans, il ne restait plus que les murs et la structure en bois. Lors de la rénovation, ils ont réussi à conserver la charpente d'origine en chêne ainsi que les sols anciens en pierre de Bourgogne, la porte d'entrée et les fenêtres. La maison offre tout le confort moderne d'un hôtel cinq étoiles sans rien perdre de son charme d'antan. Les lourds fauteuils en cuir, les radiateurs en fer forgé et le bois de chêne plusieurs fois centenaire créent une atmosphère à la fois authentique et chaleureuse. Le style de la maison est l'expression d'une foi inébranlable dans ce qui est véritable et authentique.

The oak-paneled fireplace provides an atmospheric backdrop for elegant dining. Chef Alan White has gained experience in luxury hotels in the U.K. featuring star-rated restaurants.

Der mit Eichenholz verkleidete Kamin bildet die stimmungsvolle Kulisse für elegante Abendessen: Chefkoch Alan White hat in Großbritannien Erfahrung in Luxushotels mit Sterne-Gastronomie gesammelt.

La cheminée habillée de chêne crée un décor élégant et une ambiance propice aux délicieux dîners concoctés par le chef Alan White, qui a fait ses armes dans des hôtels de luxe britanniques qui abritent des restaurants étoilés.

Chalet Eco Farm

Les Houches, France

For the past 27 years, Tim and Gaby Newman have been developing chalet projects in the Chamonix area. The couple shares a preference for organic produce and an awareness of environmental protection issues. Their Eco Farm represents the perfect symbiosis of these two passions. The Newmans spent over five years renovating the house dating from 1781. They installed a geothermal heating system and rain water capture and used as many recycled and eco-friendly materials as possible. This has given the chalet an excellent energy rating. It has been furnished with modern elements without losing any of the structure's authentic Alpine character: Antiques from the region have been combined with Italian leather sofas. The living space features large roof windows as well as double doors; from there, guests enjoy magnificent views of the woods and slopes.

Tim und Gaby Newman entwickeln seit 27 Jahren Hüttenprojekte im Skigebiet um Chamonix. Das Ehepaar teilt die Vorliebe für Lebensmittel aus biologischem Anbau und das Bewusstsein für den Umweltschutz. Ihre Eco Farm ist die perfekte Symbiose aus beiden Leidenschaften. Die Newmans haben über fünf Jahre lang das 1781 erbaute Haus renoviert und dabei nur ökofreundliche Materialien verwendet. Dank einer Erdwärmeheizung, der Nutzung von Regenwasser sowie der Verwendung möglichst vieler recycelter und umweltfreundlicher Materialien weist das Haus eine exzellente Energiebilanz auf. Die Eco Farm ist modern ausgestattet, ohne dass der authentisch alpine Charakter des Gebäudes verloren geht: Zu italienischen Ledersofas sind Antiquitäten aus der Region kombiniert. Von großen Dachflächenfenstern und Doppeltüren hat man einen herrlichen Blick auf Wälder und Pisten.

Depuis 27 ans, Tim et Gaby Newman élaborent des projets de chalets dans la région de Chamonix. Le couple partage le même amour de l'agriculture biologique et le même souci de préservation de l'environnement. Leur Eco Farm est la symbiose parfaite de ces deux passions. Il leur a fallu cinq ans pour rénover cette maison, érigée en 1781, en ne faisant appel qu'à des matériaux écologiques. Grace à un système de chauffage géothermique, la récupération des eaux pluviales et l'utilisation de matériaux recyclés ou respectueux de l'environnement, la maison est très économe en énergie. L'Eco Farm a été aménagée en utilisant des éléments modernes sans pour autant dénaturer le caractère alpin authentique du bâtiment. Par exemple, les canapés en cuir italiens ont été associés à des antiquités de la région. Le séjour présente de larges vélux et des portes-fenêtres qui donnent sur les bois environnants et les pistes.

Le Chalet des Fermes de Marie

Megève, France

The chalet is located in the heart of the hamlet Fermes de Marie, just a few minutes on foot from the center of the French winter sports resort of Megève. With a total of 4,300 square feet, the three-story house can accommodate ten guests. The owners completely renovated and refurnished this ancient farmhouse. Thanks in part to the rustic furniture made of massive old oak with a dark patina, the interior radiates the warm charm of a mountain chalet. The interior designers added sophisticated natural materials such as furs, horn, and leather, along with high-quality modern textiles. The focal point of the building is the lounge area on the lower floor, which includes a fireplace edged with oak, a dining room, and a reading corner. From the lounge, guests can wander out onto the outside terrace.

Das Chalet liegt im Weiler Fermes de Marie, nur wenige Minuten Fußweg entfernt vom Zentrum des französischen Wintersportortes Megève. Das dreigeschossige Haus bietet auf insgesamt 400 Quadratmetern Platz für zehn Gäste. Der Eigentümer hat das uralte Bauernhaus komplett renoviert und neu eingerichtet. Das Innere verbreitet den warmen Charme einer Berghütte, wofür unter anderem die rustikalen Möbel aus massivem, altem Eichenholz sorgen, die bereits eine dunkle Patina angesetzt haben. Dazu kombinierten die Einrichter edle Natur-materialien wie Pelz, Horn oder Leder, ebenso hochwertige moderne Textilien. Mittelpunkt des Gebäudes ist der Loungebereich im Untergeschoss. Dort befinden sich der von Eichenholz eingefasste Kamin, das Esszimmer und die Leseecke. Von der Lounge hat der Bewohner Zugang zur Außenterrasse.

Le chalet est situé au cœur du hameau des Fermes de Marie à quelques minutes à pied du centre de la petite ville française de sport d'hiver de Megève. La maison, qui peut accueillir dix personnes sur une surface totale de 400 mètres carrés répartie sur trois niveaux, est une ancienne ferme entièrement rénovée et redécorée par son propriétaire. À l'intérieur, on retrouve l'ambiance douce et chaleureuse d'un chalet de montagne, avec ses meubles rustiques en bois de chêne massif déjà patiné par le temps, auxquels les décorateurs ont associé des matériaux à la fois nobles et naturels comme des peaux, du cuir ainsi que des textiles modernes haut de gamme. Le salon du rez-de-chaussée constitue le cœur du bâtiment. On y trouve une cheminée habillée de bois de chêne, la salle à manger et un coin lecture. De là, les occupants peuvent se rendre sur la terrasse.

The panoramic terrace is the perfect spot for a romantic dinner.
The striking master bedroom takes up the entire second floor.

Die Panoramaterrasse lädt ein zum romantischen Dinner.
Der imposante Master-Bedroom belegt komplett das erste Geschoss.

La terrasse panoramique ne demande qu'à accueillir un dîner romantique.
L'immense chambre de maître occupe l'ensemble du premier étage.

Le Chalet

Megève, France

Located in the French department of Haute-Savoie, Le Chalet is a building complex that includes two hotel chalets as well as a private chalet with butler service. When designing the property, the owners have attached the greatest importance to the respect and integration of local traditions and knowledge, to the simplicity and genuine charm of a mountain lifestyle. As a result, the furnishings do not follow some overriding motto; instead, like an immutable Alpine mountain range, they are intended to simply stand on their own. Here, there are no distractions to prevent guests from finding inner peace and balance. However, this does not mean that guests need to make sacrifices when it comes to comfort and amenities: All rooms and suites include their own balcony or terrace with a view of the Alps. In addition, the hotel chalet has a stylishly furnished salon that serves tea in front of the fireplace every afternoon at 4:00 p.m.

Beim Le Chalet im französischen Departement Haute-Savoie handelt es sich um einen Gebäudekomplex, zu dem zwei Hotel-Chalets sowie ein privates Chalet mit Butler-Service gehören. Bei der Gestaltung des Anwesens hatten die Besitzer vor allem die Einfachheit und den unverfälschten Charme des Berglebens vor Augen. Die Einrichtung folgt deshalb keinem übergeordneten Motto, sondern soll aus Respekt vor den lokalen Traditionen wie ein unverrückbares Alpenmassiv nur für sich stehen. Nichts lenkt hier davon ab, zur inneren Ruhe und Balance zurückzufinden. Das bedeutet allerdings nicht, dass die Gäste beim Komfort und der Ausstattung Verzicht üben müssen. Alle Zimmer und Suiten haben Zugang zu einem eigenen Balkon oder einer Terrasse mit Alpenblick. Das Hotel-Chalet verfügt außerdem über einen stilvoll eingerichteten Salon, in dem jeden Nachmittag um 16 Uhr vorm Kamin zur Tea Time geladen wird.

Le Chalet est un ensemble de bâtiments situé en Haute-Savoie, comprenant deux hôtels-chalets ainsi qu'un chalet privé avec service de majordome. En imaginant le chalet, les propriétaires ont attaché la plus grand importance au respect et à l'intégration des cultures et savoir-faire locaux, au charme authentique de la vie dans les alpages. L'architecture intérieur repose sur la simplicité, elle se suffit à elle-même. Rien ne saurait empêcher les visiteurs de retrouver leur équilibre et la paix intérieure. Cela ne signifie pas pour autant que les clients doivent apprendre à renoncer au confort et aux aménagements modernes. Toutes les chambres et suites sont dotées d'un balcon ou d'une terrasse avec vue sur les Alpes. L'hôtel-chalet dispose d'un salon décoré avec goût, où, chaque après-midi à 16 heures, le thé est servi devant de la cheminée.

Chalet Les Brames

Méribel, France

In the 1990s, Chalet Les Brames near Méribel was one of the first "super chalets" in the region. At the time, luxury properties of this type were still the exception. Over the years, an increasing number of property owners constructed chalets that satisfied the modern demands for comfort and luxury. Soon some of the new constructions were so impressive that Chalet Les Brames began to run the risk of losing its status as the superstar of the region. For this reason, in 2011 the owners launched a total renovation of their property. The result no longer needs to fear competition: Today, the chalet is once again one of the most beautiful vacation homes in France. It can accommodate up to twelve guests who can enjoy furnishings of the highest quality.

Das in der Nähe von Méribel gelegene Chalet Les Brames gehörte in den 90er Jahren zu den ersten „Super-Chalets" der Region. Luxus-anwesen dieser Art waren damals noch die Ausnahme. Im Laufe der Zeit bauten allerdings immer mehr Eigentümer Hütten, die den modernen Ansprüchen an Komfort und Luxus genügten. Manche der Neubauten beeindruckten schon bald so sehr, dass das Chalet Les Brames seinen Status als Superstar der Region zu verlieren drohte. Aus diesem Grund haben die Eigentümer im Jahr 2011 damit begonnen, ihr Anwesen vom Boden bis zum Dach zu renovieren. Das Ergebnis braucht die Konkurrenz nun nicht mehr zu scheuen: Das Chalet gehört heute wieder zu den schönsten Ferienhäusern Frankreichs. Bis zu zwölf Personen finden hier Platz und dürfen eine Ausstattung allererster Güte genießen.

Dans les années 90, le Chalet Les Brames, situé dans les environs de Méribel, comptait parmi les premiers « super chalets » de la région. Les propriétés proposant un tel luxe étaient encore rares à l'époque. Au fil des ans, les chalets répondant aux critères de luxe et de confort d'une clientèle toujours plus exigeante se sont multipliés. Certaines de ces nouvelles constructions étaient si impressionnantes que le Chalet Les Brames a bien failli de cesser d'être considéré comme le chef-d'œuvre de la région. En 2011, ses propriétaires ont donc décidé de le rénover entièrement. À l'issue des travaux, la crainte de la concurrence n'était plus qu'un lointain souvenir. Le chalet compte de nouveau parmi les plus belles résidences secondaires de France. Douze personnes peuvent s'y installer et profiter d'un équipement de très haut niveau.

The interior designers drew their inspiration from modern art and used high-quality upholstered furniture in light colors. Thanks to its panoramic window, the living room feels like a part of nature.

Bei den Interieurs setzten die Einrichter auf moderne Kunst und hochwertige, helle Polstermöbel. Der Wohnzimmer-Salon wirkt dank seiner Panoramafenster wie ein Teil der Natur.

Pour les intérieurs, les décorateurs ont misé sur l'art contemporain et des meubles capitonnés clairs haut de gamme. Grâce aux fenêtres panoramiques, le salon-séjour semble intégré au paysage.

Chalet la Transhumance

Saint-Martin-de-Belleville, France

Interior designer Noé Duchaufour Lawrance completed the renovation of 5,700-square-foot Chalet la Transhumance in 2011. Although the outer façade is still reminiscent of a traditional mountain chalet, the furnishings inside reveal a completely new approach for the Alpine region. The designer chose to go with polished concrete floors, and he covered the walls with oiled gray fir and natural Vals stone. All the furniture comes from renowned designers, including Jean-Marie Massaud, Johanna Grawunder, and Ronan & Erwan Bouroullec. The main room occupies the entire upper level of the building and centers around a cylindrical fireplace suspended from the ceiling. The sides of the 215-square-foot Jacuzzi are clad in quartzite, and the water shimmers as emerald green as a mysterious mountain lake.

Der Innenarchitekt Noé Duchaufour Lawrance hat den Umbau des 530 Quadratmeter großen Chalets la Transhumance im Dezember 2011 fertiggestellt. Während die Außenfassade noch an eine traditionelle Berghütte erinnert, offenbart die Inneneinrichtung einen für die Alpenregion vollkommen neuen Ansatz. Bei den Böden wählte der Architekt blanken Betonestrich, die Wände verkleidete er mit grau geöltem Tannenholz und Valser Naturstein. Sämtliche Möbel stammen von namhaften Designern, darunter Jean-Marie Massaud, Johanna Grawunder oder Ronan & Erwan Bouroullec. Der Hauptraum umfasst die gesamte obere Etage des Gebäudes. In dessen Zentrum steht ein zylinderförmiger, von der Decke abgehängter Kamin. Das Becken des 20 Quadratmeter großen Jacuzzi ist mit Quarzit ausgekleidet. Das Wasser schimmert darin smaragdgrün wie in einem geheimnisvollen Bergsee.

L'architecte d'intérieur Noé Duchaufour Lawrance a réalisé la transformation des 530 mètres carrés du Chalet la Transhumance en décembre 2011. Tandis que la façade rappelle toujours un chalet de montagne traditionnel, l'intérieur révèle un concept complètement nouveau pour cette région des Alpes. L'architecte a choisi d'habiller les sols d'une chape de béton poli et les murs de sapin gris huilé et de pierre de Vals. L'ensemble du mobilier a été conçu par de célèbres designers, dont Jean-Marie Massaud, Johanna Grawunder et Ronan & Erwan Bouroullec. La salle principale occupe l'intégralité de l'étage supérieur du bâtiment. Une cheminée cylindrique est suspendue au plafond au centre de la pièce. Les 20 mètres carrés du bassin du jacuzzi sont revêtus de quartzite. Les reflets vert émeraude de l'eau évoquent la surface d'un mystérieux lac de montagne.

House in Val d'Isère

Val d'Isère, France

This chalet is located in the heart of Val d'Isère not far from ski runs, restaurants, and stores. The amenities include six bedrooms and baths, a fireplace, billiard table, home theater, steam bath, and massage room. Nicky Dobree was responsible for designing the interior. A specialist in designing upscale mountain chalets, Dobree uses warm earth tones and sophisticated natural materials, such as furs, leather, and stone. This designer also refashions typical design elements of the Alpine chalet: She creates chandeliers out of hunting trophies and covers armchairs and ottomans with animal hides. The use of plaid fabrics reflects her typical British style. In this fashion, Dobree blends the dignified refinement of a British parlor with the charm of a rustic mountain chalet.

Das Chalet befindet sich im Herzen der Gemeinde Val d'Isère, in nächster Nähe zu Skipisten, Restaurants und Läden. Zur Ausstattung gehören sechs Schlafzimmer und Bäder, Kamin, Billardtisch, Kino, Dampfbad und Massageraum. Für die Inneneinrichtung zeichnet Nicky Dobree verantwortlich. Die auf die Gestaltung hochwertiger Bergchalets spezialisierte Designerin setzt auf erdige, warme Farbtöne und edle Naturmaterialien wie Pelz, Leder oder Stein. Typische Gestaltungselemente der alpinen Hütte funktioniert die Designerin um. So fertigt sie aus Jagdtrophäen Leuchten, Sessel und Poufs bezieht sie mit Tierfellen. Auf ihren typisch britischen Stil verweisen die Karomuster der Textilien. Dobree verbindet auf diese Weise die gediegene Vornehmheit des englischen Salons mit dem Charme einer urigen Berghütte.

Ce chalet est situé au cœur de la commune de Val d'Isère, à deux pas des pistes, des restaurants et des commerces. Il est pourvu de six chambres avec salles de bain, d'une cheminée, d'un billard, d'une salle de cinéma, d'un hammam et d'une salle de massage. La décoration intérieure est signée Nicky Dobree. La décoratrice, spécialisée dans les chalets haut de gamme, affectionne les tons chauds et terreux, ainsi que les matériaux naturels comme les peaux, le cuir ou la pierre. Elle détourne aussi volontiers les éléments de décoration typiquement montagnards, en créant des lustres à partir de trophée de chasse ou en recouvrant de fourrure les poufs et fauteuils. Les motifs à carreaux des textiles témoignent de son héritage britannique. Dobree réunit ainsi l'élégance bourgeoise d'un salon anglais et le charme d'un authentique chalet de montagne.

Farmer's tables and benches are traditional furnishings in Alpine mountain chalets—here they are a Pugin inspired design crafted in seasoned French oak. With its sophisticated lounge furniture and a fireplace, the living room offers a culture of luxury at its finest.

Bauerntisch und Bank sind traditionelle Einrichtungselemente der alpinen Berghütte – sie wurden für das Chalet aus alter französischer Eiche gefertigt, inspiriert vom neogotischen Design Pugins. Das Wohnzimmer bietet mit seinen edlen Loungemöbeln und dem Kamin luxuriöse Salonkultur.

Une table de ferme et des bancs font partie du mobilier traditionnel des chalets alpins – ici le design s'est inspiré de Pugin et les pièces ont été fabriquées en vieux chêne français. La salle de séjour propose une déclinaison luxueuse du salon grâce à des meubles haut de gamme et une belle cheminée.

BergLodge

Nesselwang, Germany

Ludwig Böck is the father of the BergLodge in Nesselwang, Germany. Following his career, this Allgäu athlete and former Olympian opened a clubhouse for sports enthusiasts which quickly became one of the favorite hangouts in the region. In 2008, the building complex was converted into four exclusive lodges. At an elevation of 5,000 feet, the property also includes three restaurants and a large panoramic terrace. Each lodge is comfortably equipped with a fireplace and its own sauna. A special highlight included in the amenities of each lodge is a wine refrigerator. In the bedrooms, beds with American box springs provide for restful sleep. Guests can enjoy a refreshing drink of mountain spring water from the lodge's very own spring.

Ludwig Böck ist der Vater der BergLodge im deutschen Nesselwang. Der Allgäuer Sportler und Olympia-Teilnehmer eröffnete nach seiner Karriere ein Sportlerheim, das sich schnell zu einem der beliebtesten Treffpunkte der Region entwickelte. 2008 erfolgte der Umbau des Gebäudekomplexes zu vier exklusiven Lodges. Das Anwesen liegt in einer Höhe von 1 500 Metern und besteht zusätzlich aus drei Gaststuben und einer großen Panoramaterrasse. Jede Lodge verfügt über eine komfortable Ausstattung mit Kamin und eigener Sauna. Ein besonderes Highlight ist der Weinklimaschrank, der zur Einrichtung jeder Lodge gehört. In den Schlafzimmern sorgen amerikanische Boxspringbetten für erholsamen Schlaf. Wohltuende Erfrischung finden die Gäste bei einem Schluck Bergquellwasser aus dem hauseigenen Brunnen.

Ludwig Böck a donné vie au BergLodge en Allemagne du côté de Nesselwang à 1 500 mètres d'altitude. Natif de l'Allgäu, cet ancien sportif a fait partie de l'équipe olympique de son pays. Au terme de sa carrière, il a décidé d'ouvrir un centre pour sportifs qui est rapidement devenu l'un des plus plébiscités dans la région. En 2008, le complexe a été transformé pour en faire quatre pavillons d'exception, auxquels il faut ajouter trois salles de restaurant et une vaste terrasse panoramique. Chaque pavillon est équipé de tout le confort, cheminée et sauna y compris, mais aussi d'une spécificité: une armoire cave à vin. Dans les chambres, les lits boxspring garantissent un sommeil réparateur. Les clients peuvent se rafraîchir en profitant des bienfaits de l'eau de source qui coule directement à la fontaine du complexe.

Craftsmen used natural stone in the bathrooms. Walls and ceilings covered in
Alpine stone pine provide a healthy room climate that lowers the heart rate.

Bei der Gestaltung des Bads arbeiteten die Einrichter mit Naturstein.
Die aus dem Holz der alpinen Zirbelkiefer gefertigten Decken und Wände
sorgen für ein gesundes, herzfrequenzsenkendes Raumklima.

Les décorateurs travaillent avec de la pierre naturelle pour l'aménagement de
la salle de bain. Le pin cembro typique des Alpes, qui recouvre les plafonds
et les murs, contribue à un environnement intérieur sain et apaisant.

San Lorenzo Mountain Lodge
St. Lorenzen, Dolomites, Italy

Whenever Giorgia and Stefano Barbini needed to take a break from their hectic business life in Rome, they would be drawn to the mountains of South Tyrol. On one of these trips, they discovered the "Unterramwaldhof," a neglected chalet high above St. Lorenzen at an elevation of 4,000 feet. There the Barbinis immediately decided to fulfill their dream of creating a mountain retreat. Dating back to the 16th century, this hunting chalet offers something unusual at this elevation: a generous layout and extensive sophisticated woodwork on the doors and paneling. The vaulted renaissance ceiling in the entrance hall is a reminder of its original use as a residence for an aristocratic family. With a sure hand, the owners have breathed new life into the ancient rooms, successfully creating a wonderful symbiosis of an ancient and modern lifestyle.

Immer wenn Giorgia und Stefano Barbini sich eine Auszeit von ihrem hektischen Geschäftsleben in Rom gönnten, zog es sie in die Südtiroler Berge. Auf einem dieser Ausflüge entdeckten sie hoch über St. Lorenzen, auf 1 200 Metern Höhe, den verwahrlosten „Unterramwaldhof". Die Barbinis beschlossen sofort, sich an diesem Ort ihren Traum vom zurückgezogenen Leben in den Bergen zu verwirklichen. Das aus dem 16. Jahrhundert stammende Jagdchalet bietet – ungewöhnlich in dieser Höhe – einen großzügigen Grundriss und viele raffinierte Holzarbeiten an Türen und Täfelung. Auch die Renaissance-Gewölbedecke der Eingangshalle verweist auf die ursprüngliche Nutzung als Adelssitz. Stilsicher hauchten die Eigentümer den antiken Räumen neues Leben ein. Ihnen gelang dabei eine wunderbare Symbiose aus uraltem und modernem Wohnen.

Lorsque Giorgia et Stefano Barbini s'offraient quelques jours de repos pour récupérer de leur vie professionnelle haletante à Rome, ils se retiraient toujours dans les montagnes du Tyrol du Sud. Lors de l'un de ces séjours, ils découvrirent « Unterramwaldhof », un bâtiment à l'abandon au-dessus de San Lorenzo, à 1 200 mètres d'altitude. Les Barbini décidèrent de suite d'y réaliser leur rêve : une retraite au cœur des montagnes. Chose exceptionnelle à cette altitude, le chalet de chasse du XVIe siècle dispose de vastes pièces et comporte de nombreuses boiseries raffinées sur les portes et les lambris. De plus, le plafond voûté du hall d'entrée, qui date de la Renaissance, témoigne de la noblesse initiale du lieu. Les propriétaires ont insufflé avec goût une nouvelle vie aux pièces anciennes. Ils ont marié avec brio l'habitat moderne à la tradition.

Pale wood wainscoting in the living area creates the cozy feel of a mountain chalet, while simultaneously setting the stage for contemporary furniture with vibrant blue upholstery or striking fur coverings. A set of antlers, rough plastered walls, and knots in old wood bring the hunting chalet's nearly 500-year history to life.

Helle Holzvertäfelungen im Wohnbereich vermitteln die Behaglichkeit einer Berghütte und schaffen gleichzeitig den richtigen Rahmen für zeitgemäße Polstermöbel in kräftigem Blau oder mit auffälligem Fellbezug. Ein Geweih, grob verputzte Wände und Astlöcher in altem Holz lassen die fast 500-jährige Geschichte des Jagdchalets aufleben.

Les boiseries claires dans le séjour évoquent la chaleur rassurante d'une maison de montagne et soulignent en même temps les formes contemporaines des canapés bleu intense ou revêtus de peaux. Les ramures accrochées sur les murs enduits et les nœuds dans le bois ancien font revivre l'histoire de ce chalet cinq fois centenaire.

Mountain Lodge Trysil
Trøgstad, Norway

During the construction of their chalet, the owners had to solve a complex problem. Although they intended to use the building themselves as a vacation home, the family also wanted to rent it. As a result, the furnishings had to be practical while also offering a sense of homey intimacy. In addition, it had to provide enough sleeping accommodations for everyone. In the end, the family planned a building with a total of eight bedrooms and three bathrooms. Owner Kjartan Dahl built most of the house himself, although he turned to a professional architect to handle the planning. The family also sought out a specialist for the interior. Helene Hennie, a well-known interior designer in Norway and the recipient of numerous awards, handled the decor.

Beim Bau ihrer Berghütte mussten die Besitzer eine komplexe Aufgabe lösen. Sie hatten die Absicht, das Gebäude als Ferienhaus selbst zu nutzen. Ebenso wollte die Familie die Hütte aber auch vermieten. Die Einrichtung sollte deshalb praktisch sein, aber auch ein Gefühl von heimischer Intimität bieten. Außerdem mussten ausreichend Schlafplätze vorhanden sein. Am Ende plante die Familie ein Gebäude mit insgesamt acht Schlafräumen und drei Badezimmern. Erbaut hat das Haus der Besitzer Kjartan Dahl größtenteils in Eigenarbeit, wobei ein professioneller Architekt die Planung übernommen hat. Bei der Inneneinrichtung verließ sich die Familie ebenfalls auf fachmännische Hilfe. Die in Norwegen bekannte und mit vielen Preisen ausgezeichnete Innenarchitektin Helene Hennie hat die Interieurs gestaltet.

Pour construire leur chalet de montagne, les propriétaires de ce lieu ont dû résoudre une équation difficile : ils souhaitaient à la fois pouvoir profiter de la maison en tant que résidence secondaire et la louer en leur absence. La décoration devait donc être pratique tout en donnant une sensation d'intimité, comme celle d'un vrai foyer. De plus, il fallait proposer des lits en suffisance. Finalement, la famille a conçu un bâtiment comptant au total huit chambres à coucher et trois salles de bain. Le propriétaire, Kjartan Dahl, s'est chargé dans une large mesure de la construction de la maison, mais a confié la réalisation des plans à un architecte de métier. En matière de décoration, la famille s'est également reposée sur les conseils avertis de professionnels, en faisant appel à Helene Hennie, une architecte d'intérieur titulaire de nombreux prix.

*Because Scandinavians love to surround themselves with wood,
the fireplace is built out of light spruce wood instead of stone.*

*Die Skandinavier wohnen gerne mit viel Holz. Der Kamin ist
deshalb nicht mit Stein, sondern mit hellem Fichtenholz eingefasst.*

*Les Scandinaves aiment intégrer le bois dans leur habitat ; raison pour
laquelle, la cheminée n'est pas revêtue de pierre, mais d'épicéa clair.*

The Villa at Copperhill Mountain Lodge

Åre, Sweden

The slopes of the Åreskutan plateau belong to some of the largest and most beautiful ski areas in Sweden. Copperhill Mountain Lodge is located high up on the mountain, above Åre village and lake with access to the slopes. Since 2010, this property of Nordic Choice Hotels and member of Design Hotels, has extended an exclusive offer to its guests: They can rent the luxurious private lodge of Norwegian hotel magnate Petter A. Stordalen. The lodge is simply called "The Villa" and with eight bedrooms can accommodate a total of 16 guests. The 7,500-square-foot wooden house features state-of-the-art architecture with furniture and light fixtures from notable contemporary designers. Norwegian designer Anemone Wille Våge handled the interior; her projects include furnishing the private apartments of the Norwegian royal couple.

Die Hänge der Åreskutan-Hochebene gehören zu den schönsten und größten Skigebieten Schwedens. Hoch auf dem Berg, über dem Ort Åre und seinem See, befindet sich die Copperhill Mountain Lodge mit Zugang zu den Pisten. Seit 2010 macht das Mitglied von Nordic Choice Hotels und der Designhotel-Gruppe seinen Besuchern ein exklusives Angebot. Die Gäste können die luxuriöse, private Lodge des norwegischen Hotel-Magnaten Petter A. Stordalen mieten. Der Name der Lodge lautet einfach „Die Villa". Acht Schlafzimmer stehen für 16 Gäste zur Verfügung. Das 700 Quadratmeter große Holzhaus bietet modernste Architektur und ist mit Möbeln und Leuchten namhafter, zeitgenössischer Designer eingerichtet. Verantwortlich für das Interieur ist die norwegische Designerin Anemone Wille Våge, die auch die privaten Räume des norwegischen Königspaars ausgestattet hat.

Sur les pentes du plateau Åreskutan se trouve l'une des plus belles et des plus grandes stations de ski de Suède. Situé sur les hauteurs de Åre et de son lac, Copperhill Mountain Lodge offre un accès direct aux pistes. Depuis 2010, cet hôtel, membre du groupe Nordic Choice Hotels et Design Hotel, propose à ses clients quelque chose d'exceptionnel. Ils peuvent en effet louer le lodge du magnat norvégien de l'hôtellerie, Petter A. Stordalen. Son nom est un exemple de simplicité : « la villa ». Cette maison en bois, de 700 mètres carrés, à l'architecture résolument contemporaine, comprend huit chambres et peut accueillir 16 hôtes. L'aménagement qui fait appel à des meubles et à des luminaires de célèbres designers contemporains a été confié à la décoratrice norvégienne Anemone Wille Våge, qui a notamment signé la décoration des appartements privés du couple royal norvégien.

Pelts in the living and sleeping area exemplify luxury and create an atmosphere of comfort and warmth. The candlelight, which seems to float on a shelf above the dining table, contributes to this ambience.

Felle im Wohn- und Schlafbereich stehen für Luxus und vermitteln gleichzeitig Wärme und Behaglichkeit. Dazu trägt auch das Kerzenlicht bei, das auf einem Bord über dem Esstisch zu schweben scheint.

Les peaux dans les chambres et le séjour témoignent du luxe des lieux et suscitent en même temps une douce sensation de bien-être, soulignée par les bougies qui semblent flotter sur une planche au-dessus de la table de la salle à manger.

Chalet Rougemont

Gstaad Valley, Switzerland

The two resident interior designers Federica and Tamara Sessa completely furnished this chalet located in the Alpine village of Rougemont. Traditional wood construction methods were used for the entire house. For the interior design, however, Tamara's Design favored modern design elements and maximum comfort rather than the simple chalet look. Custom-made beds in the bedrooms ensure a good night's sleep in a stylish ambience. All furniture in antique wood has been conceived by Tamara's Design and crafted by a local carpentry shop. The salon features straight, classic lines, providing predominantly sophisticated gray tones combined with black-and-white contrasts.

Die beiden ortsansässigen Innenarchitektinnen Federica und Tamara Sessa haben das im Alpendorf Rougemont gelegene Chalet komplett eingerichtet. Das gesamte Haus ist auf traditionelle Weise aus Holz gebaut. Bei der Einrichtung setzte Tamara's Design allerdings nicht mehr auf den einfachen Hüttenlook, sondern auf moderne Gestaltungselemente und hohen Wohnkomfort. In den Schlafzimmern sorgen maßgefertigte Betten für nächtliche Erholung in stilvollem Ambiente. Sämtliches Mobiliar aus antikem Holz stammt aus der Feder von Tamara's Design, eigens für das Chalet entworfen und in der örtlichen Tischlerei angefertigt. Der Salon ist durchweg von geraden, klassischen Linien geprägt. Bei den Farben dominieren elegante Grautöne sowie Schwarz-Weiß-Kontraste.

Federica et Tamara Sessa, toutes deux architectes d'intérieur, ont entièrement redécoré ce chalet situé dans le village alpin de Rougemont. L'ensemble de la maison est construit en bois et de façon traditionnelle. En matière d'aménagement en revanche, Tamara's Design ne recherchait pas une simple ambiance de chalet, mais plutôt des éléments de décoration contemporains associés à un grand confort. Les chambres à coucher disposent de lits conçus sur mesure pour créer une ambiance propice à de véritables nuits de repos. L'ensemble du mobilier, qui porte la griffe de Tamara's Design, a été conçu spécialement pour le chalet, puis réalisé par des ébénistes locaux en bois ancien. Le salon adopte des lignes classiques et pures. Dans le choix des couleurs, ce sont les contrastes noir et blanc, ainsi qu'un beau camaïeu de gris qui dominent.

Guests will enjoy contemporary design in the puristic bathroom.
The fixtures come from a product line by the Italian brand Gessi.

Auch im puristisch gestalteten Bad findet der Bewohner zeitgenössisches Design.
Die Armaturen stammen aus einer Produktlinie der italienischen Firma Gessi.

La salle de bain très épurée fait également appel au design contemporain.
La robinetterie provient de la marque italienne Gessi.

Chesa Farrer

Celerina, Switzerland

Chesa Farrer is one of several traditional Engadin farmhouses in the center of the village of Celerina. The buildings date from the 17th century and have been transformed for modern use. Chesa Farrer was used as a farmhouse until the early 20th century; afterwards, the owners expanded the building into an inn with a restaurant. In 1988, however, the owners carried out some radical changes. They installed concrete walls, relocated the kitchen to the street side, and built an additional staircase. The current owner removed all of these modifications and restored the original spacious room layout. Craftsmen even restored the old walls and woodwork to reflect their original appearance.

Die Chesa Farrer gehört zu einer Gruppe traditioneller Engadiner Bauernhäuser im Zentrum des Dorfes Celerina. Die Gebäude stammen alle aus dem 17. Jahrhundert und sind heute in eine moderne Nutzung überführt. Bis zum Beginn des 20. Jahrhunderts war die Chesa Farrer als Bauernhaus bewohnt. Danach bauten die Besitzer das Gebäude zu einem Gasthof mit Restaurant aus. Im Jahr 1988 nahmen die damaligen Eigentümer abermals einige radikale Veränderungen vor. Sie zogen Betonwände ein, verlegten die Küche zur Straßenseite und errichteten einen zusätzlichen Treppenaufgang. Der heutige Hausherr hat diese Eingriffe alle entfernt und die ursprüngliche, großzügige Raumaufteilung wiederhergestellt. Auch das alte Mauerwerk sowie die Holzarbeiten haben Handwerker originalgetreu restauriert.

La maison Chesa Farrer fait partie d'un groupe de fermes traditionnelles de l'Engadine, situé au cœur du bourg de Celerina. Les bâtiments datent tous du XVIIᵉ siècle et sont désormais conformes aux attentes d'aujourd'hui en matière d'habitat. La maison Chesa Farrer fut habitée jusqu'au début du XXᵉ siècle, avant d'être agrandie et transformée en auberge. En 1988, les propriétaires de l'époque entreprirent des transformations radicales. Ils élevèrent des cloisons de béton, déplacèrent la cuisine côté rue et érigèrent un escalier supplémentaire. L'actuel maître des lieux a supprimé toutes ces interventions, puis rétabli la répartition initiale des pièces en leur redonnant tout leur espace. Grâce au travail des artisans, l'ancienne maçonnerie et les boiseries ont retrouvé leur aspect original.

Julierhof

Champfèr, Switzerland

When Julierhof was built in 1869 as a small luxury hotel, it had a fabulous view toward the village of Maloja. Over the years, the area has been built up and the views are no longer quite as open, but the residents can still see the peaceful mountain peaks of the Engadin valley. The house stood empty for years until the current owners began renovations. Their goal was to completely retain the original structure. They had massive pine planks laid on the floors to create a cozy atmosphere even in the winter. The walls feature a simple white plaster. The deep window recesses show how thick the walls originally were. The style of the decoration has also been kept simple and plain. Some of the old drapes had to be removed to create a better setting for the collection of contemporary art.

Der Julierhof war ursprünglich eines kleines, 1869 erbautes Luxushotel mit wunderbarem Blick in Richtung des Dorfes Maloja. Inzwischen ist in der Gegend viel gebaut worden und die Aussicht nicht mehr ganz so frei. Auf die in sich ruhenden Berggipfel des Engadins schauen die Bewohner aber heute noch. Das Haus stand lange Zeit leer, bis die jetzigen Besitzer mit der Sanierung begonnen haben. Die ursprüngliche Baustruktur wollten die Eigentümer komplett erhalten. Auf den Böden haben sie massive Kiefernbohlen verlegt, um auch im Winter eine behagliche Atmosphäre zu schaffen. Die Wände sind einfach weiß verputzt. Die tiefen Laibungen der Fenster zeigen, wie dick die Wände ursprünglich gewesen sind. Schlicht und klar gehalten ist auch der Stil der Dekoration. Einige der alten Vorhänge mussten verschwinden, damit die Sammlung zeitgenössischer Kunst besser zur Geltung kommt.

Construit en 1869, le Julierhof était à l'origine un petit hôtel de luxe qui offrait une vue merveilleuse sur le village de Maloja. Depuis, le quartier s'est considérablement bâti et la vue n'est plus aussi dégagée qu'auparavant. Néanmoins, les occupants peuvent toujours contempler les paisibles sommets de l'Engadine. La maison est restée vide pendant des années jusqu'au moment où le propriétaire actuel s'est lancé dans des rénovations, avec l'intention, toutefois, de garder la structure originale. Les sols ont été revêtus d'un plancher en pin massif afin de créer une ambiance accueillante en hiver. Les murs ont été enduits d'un simple plâtre blanc. La profondeur des fenêtres témoigne de l'épaisseur originale des murs. Le style de la décoration est lui aussi resté simple et épuré. Quelques-uns des anciens rideaux ont dû être retirés pour mettre en valeur la collection d'art contemporain.

A painting of world-famous German artist A.R. Penck hangs above the sofa, and the many
art books on the coffee table bear witness to the fact that an art lover lives here.

Über dem Sofa hängt ein Bild des weltberühmten deutschen Künstlers A.R. Penck. Auch die vielen
Bildbände auf dem Couchtisch sind ein Beleg dafür, dass hier ein Kunstliebhaber zu Hause ist.

Au-dessus du canapé trône un tableau de l'artiste allemand de renommée mondiale A.R. Penck.
De même, les nombreux livres présents sur la table basse témoignent de l'habitat d'un amateur d'art.

Chesa Alta

La Punt, Switzerland

Chesa Alta is the largest building in La Punt and dates back to 1620. In more recent decades, pharmaceutical company Sandoz used the house as vacation lodgings for its managers and executives. Between 2001 and 2003, the current owners worked with Swiss architects to renovate the building from the ground up. With tremendous respect for its historical heritage, the owners integrated modern living standards into the ancient building. Craftsmen from the region meticulously restored all of the wooden structures. Where they had to replace structural components, they used only local materials. Thanks to this careful restoration, it is now possible to see the craftsmanship and treasures the region has produced over the centuries. Today, Chesa Alta is more than just a ski chalet—it is a house to be enjoyed year round.

Die Chesa Alta ist das größte Gebäude in La Punt und stammt aus dem Jahr 1620. In der neueren Zeit nutzte der Pharmakonzern Sandoz das Haus als Ferienunterkunft für seine Führungskräfte. In den Jahren 2001 bis 2003 renovierte der jetzige Besitzer in Zusammenarbeit mit Architekten aus der Schweiz das Gebäude von Grund auf. Mit großem Respekt vor der historischen Grundsubstanz haben die Eigentümer moderne Wohnstandards in das uralte Gebäude integriert. Handwerker aus der Region haben sämtliche Holzkonstruktionen sorgfältig restauriert. Wenn sie Bauteile ersetzen mussten, verwendeten sie ausschließlich lokale Materialien. Dank der aufwendigen Restaurierung ist sichtbar, welche handwerklichen Schätze die Region über Jahrhunderte hervorgebracht hat. Die Chesa Alta ist heute keine reine Skihütte, sondern ein Haus für das ganze Jahr.

Érigée en 1620, la Chesa Alta est le plus grand bâtiment de La Punt. Il y a encore quelques années, il servait de logement de vacances pour le personnel de direction du groupe pharmaceutique Sandoz. De 2001 à 2003, le propriétaire actuel a entièrement rénové le bâtiment, en collaboration avec des architectes suisses. Les maîtres des lieux ont veillé à pourvoir ces vieilles pierres de tout le confort que requiert un habitat contemporain, tout en respectant l'héritage qu'elles représentent. Des artisans de la région ont restauré avec précaution l'ensemble de la charpente, en recourant exclusivement à des matériaux locaux lorsque des éléments devaient être remplacés. Ce travail minutieux a permis de mettre en valeur des trésors d'artisanat produits dans cette région depuis des siècles. La Chesa Alta n'est plus une simple résidence de vacances d'hiver, mais bien une maison pour toutes les saisons.

The magnificent vaulted ceilings bear witness to the building's long history.
The owners used many antiques from the Baroque era in the interior furnishings.

Die prachtvollen Gewölbedecken zeugen von der uralten Historie des Gebäudes.
Bei der Einrichtung verwendeten die Besitzer viele Antiquitäten aus dem Barock.

Les majestueux plafonds voûtés témoignent de l'histoire séculaire du bâtiment. Pour la
décoration, les propriétaires ont utilisé de nombreuses antiquités de l'époque baroque.

House in Les Collons

Les Collons, Switzerland

Thanks to its furnishings alone, this mountain chalet constructed in Les Collons in 2010 is more than just a ski lodge. Four bedrooms and baths as well as a fitness room await guests. The kitchen, living room, and dining area are located on the upper level. All rooms offer spectacular views of snow-capped peaks and the nearby Val d'Hérémence. London designer Nicky Dobree created the interior. Dobree's interpretation puts a contemporary twist on the traditional Alpine style by using custom-made pieces of furniture from old wood in a modern design. Sophisticated fabrics and textiles, such as furs, wool, and linen, create a sense of coziness. Thanks to this successful combination, guests at the chalet can experience mountain life and its traditions without having to give up any of the amenities of modern living.

Alleine schon wegen seiner Ausstattung ist das 2010 erbaute Bergchalet in Les Collons mehr als nur eine Skihütte. Den Bewohnern stehen vier Schlafzimmer und Bäder sowie ein Fitnessraum zur Verfügung. In der oberen Etage befinden sich Küche, Wohn- und Essbereich. Alle Zimmer bieten spektakuläre Blicke auf schneebedeckte Gipfel und das nahe Val d'Hérémence. Nicky Dobree aus London hat die Innen-einrichtung gestaltet. Die Designerin interpretiert auf zeitgenössische Weise den traditionellen Alpenstil, indem sie bei den Möbeln zum Beispiel auf maßgefertigte Stücke aus altem Holz in modernem Design zurückgreift. Dazu schaffen edle Wohntextilien aus Pelz, Wolle oder Leinen Behaglichkeit. Dank dieser gelungenen Kombination erleben die Bewohner des Chalets die Bergwelt und deren Traditionen, ohne dabei auf die Annehmlichkeiten des modernen Wohnens verzichten zu müssen.

La richesse de l'équipement indique déjà que ce chalet de montagne, construit en 2010 aux Collons, est bien plus qu'un simple hébergement pour skieurs. Les occupants disposent de quatre chambres avec salles de bains et d'une salle de sport. Toutes les chambres offrent une vue spectaculaire sur les sommets enneigés et le Val d'Hérémence tout proche. À l'étage supérieur se trouvent la cuisine, ainsi que la zone salle à manger-séjour. La Londonienne Nicky Dobree, qui a été chargée de la décoration intérieure, a revisité le style alpin traditionnel en intégrant des éléments contemporains en bois vieilli, conçus sur mesure. De plus, le recours à des revêtements nobles comme les peaux, la laine ou le lin, produit un sentiment de plénitude. Grâce à cette combinaison réussie, les occupants du chalet font l'expérience de la montagne et de ses traditions sans renoncer aux commodités de l'habitat moderne.

Chesa Cresta

St. Moritz, Switzerland

Chesa Cresta was built in 1958 by Mario Verdieri, an architect well-known in the Engadin valley. The current owners initially lived in the villa in its original state for a year. This time enabled them to thoroughly study the light and the atmosphere in the house at different times of day, which helped shape their renovation. The exterior façade was retained in its entirety during the building's renovation. Most of the furnishings in Chesa Cresta come from Veneto, a region in Northern Italy. While exploring old farmhouses there, the owners discovered beautiful antique furniture and fixtures. The decorations are quite Baroque: sophisticated velvets, floral designs, old landscape paintings, and drapes featuring artistic embroidery. The large cabinet in the living room contains a valuable collection of Biedermeier glasses.

Der im Engadin sehr bekannte Architekt Mario Verdieri hat die Chesa Cresta 1958 erbaut. Die jetzigen Besitzer haben die Villa zunächst ein Jahr lang im ursprünglichen Zustand bewohnt. In dieser Zeit haben sie ausgiebig das Licht und die Atmosphäre zu den verschiedenen Tageszeiten studieren können, was in die Renovierung einfloss. Bei der Neugestaltung des Gebäudes blieb die Außenfassade komplett erhalten. Die Inneneinrichtung der Chesa Cresta stammt in großen Teilen aus der norditalienischen Region Venetien. Die Eigentümer entdeckten dort in alten Bauernstuben wunderschöne antike Möbel und Einrichtungsgegenstände. Die Dekoration fällt sehr barock aus. Man findet edle Samte, Blumendekore, alte Landschaftsgemälde sowie Vorhänge mit kunstvollen Stickereien. Der große Wandschrank im Wohnzimmer beinhaltet eine wertvolle Sammlung von Biedermeiergläsern.

L'architecte Mario Verdieri, célèbre dans la région d'Engadine, a construit la Chesa Cresta en 1958. Les propriétaires actuels ont habité la villa dans son état original pendant un an. Durant cette période, ils ont étudié dans le détail la lumière et l'atmosphère qui y régnaient à toute heure du jour et en ont tenu compte lors de la rénovation. La façade extérieure, restée intacte lors du réaménagement de l'édifice, abrite un décor intérieur provenant principalement de la région de la Vénétie, au nord de l'Italie. Les propriétaires y ont découvert de magnifiques meubles antiques et objets de décoration provenant d'anciens salons paysans. Tout ceci confère à l'endroit un style baroque composé de velours délicats, motifs floraux, vieilles peintures de paysages et de rideaux aux broderies ouvragées. La grande armoire murale du salon contient une précieuse collection de verres de la période Biedermeier.

Chesa Musi

St. Moritz, Switzerland

During the construction of Chesa Musi, the owner placed great emphasis on the selection of the materials. They needed to be as natural as possible and also reflect the regional building tradition. As a result, the house is built completely of natural stone and wood. The architecture of the building enters into a direct dialog with the magnificent surroundings. Wherever possible, the architects installed floor-to-ceiling expanses of glass instead of solid walls. As a result, guests can enjoy spectacular panoramic views of nearby St. Moritz valley and the snow-topped alpine peaks from virtually anywhere in the house. Contemporary design classics dominate the interior furnishings. The living room with its generously sized sofa and two lounge chairs by Charles Eames offers plenty of space to relax. In the dining area, guests can sit on chairs by cult Danish designer Hans J. Wegner.

Beim Bau der Chesa Musi legte der Besitzer großen Wert auf die Auswahl der Materialien. Sie sollten möglichst natürlich sein und der Bautradition der Region entsprechen. Das Haus ist deshalb komplett aus Naturstein und Holz gebaut. Die Architektur des Gebäudes ist eine direkte Auseinandersetzung mit der großartigen Umgebung. Wo immer es möglich war, haben die Architekten die Wandflächen voll verglast. Der Bewohner genießt deshalb überall im Haus spektakuläre Panoramen auf das nahe St. Moritz-Tal und die schneebedeckten Alpengipfel. Bei der Inneneinrichtung dominieren moderne Möbelklassiker. Viel Platz zum Entspannen bietet das Wohnzimmer mit den beiden Loungechairs von Charles Eames und der großzügigen Sofalandschaft. Zum Essen nehmen die Bewohner Platz auf Stühlen des dänischen Kultdesigners Hans J. Wegner.

Lors de la construction de la maison Chesa Musi, le propriétaire a accordé une grande importance au choix des matériaux, en recourant aussi souvent que possible à des matériaux naturels et correspondant aux méthodes de construction de la région. La maison est donc entièrement construite en pierre naturelle et en bois. L'architecture du bâtiment s'inspire directement de la majesté des environs. Les architectes ont multiplié les vitrages, partout où cela a été possible. Le maître des lieux bénéficie ainsi, dans l'ensemble de la maison, d'un panorama spectaculaire sur la vallée de Saint-Moritz toute proche et sur les sommets enneigés des Alpes. En matière de décoration intérieure, les classiques du mobilier contemporain sont omniprésents. Dans le vaste séjour, la détente est assurée par deux fauteuils de Charles Eames et d'immenses canapés. Lors des repas, les occupants prennent place sur des chaises signées Hans J. Wegner, une pointure du design danois.

Chesa Nova

St. Moritz, Switzerland

Well-known Engadin architect Mario Verdieri built this beautifully situated chalet directly above Lake St. Moritz in 1941. Over the years and through many renovations and additions, the owner's family has transformed the structure into a contemporary and comfortable chalet with a relaxed atmosphere. Dating back to the 16th century, the ceiling as well as many built-ins are made of Swiss stone pine. This type of pine is also referred to as the "Queen of the Alps" because it is ideally suited to the climatic conditions of high Alpine regions. The fragrance of the wood has been proven to have positive effects on a person's health and sense of well-being. The owners carried out the last major redesign with the help of architect Heino Stamm. During the project, Stamm combined antique elements made of stone and wood with animal furs and felt upholstery materials.

Der bekannte Engadiner Architekt Mario Verdieri hat dieses wunderschön gelegene Chalet direkt über dem St. Moritzersee 1941 erbaut. Die Besitzerfamilie hat über mehrere Jahre mit vielen Um- und Anbauten das Haus in ein zeitgemäßes, gemütliches Chalet mit ungezwungener Atmosphäre verwandelt. Die aus dem 16. Jahrhundert stammende Decke sowie viele Einbauten sind aus Arvenholz gefertigt. Die Kiefernart wird auch „Königin der Alpen" genannt, da sie ideal an die klimatischen Bedingungen im hochalpinen Gelände angepasst ist. Der typische Duft des Holzes hat nachweislich positive Effekte auf das Wohlbefinden und die Gesundheit. Die letzte große Neugestaltung haben die Besitzer mithilfe des Architekten Heino Stamm durchgeführt. Zu diesem Anlass kombinierte er antike Elemente aus Stein oder Holz mit Tierfellen und Polstermaterialien aus Filz.

En 1941, Mario Verdieri, célèbre architecte de l'Engadine, a construit ce chalet magnifiquement situé sur les hauteurs du lac de Saint-Moritz. Au fil des ans, la famille propriétaire a réalisé plusieurs séries de transformations et d'extensions pour créer aujourd'hui un chalet accueillant, en phase avec son époque, où règne une atmosphère décontractée. À l'instar de nombreux aménagements encastrés, les plafonds du XVIe siècle sont réalisés en bois d'arole, une variété de conifères aussi appelée « le roi des Alpes » en raison de sa résistance aux conditions climatiques en haute montagne. Le parfum typique du bois a des effets prouvés sur la sensation de bien-être et sur la santé. L'architecte Heino Stamm a assisté les propriétaires pour réaliser la dernière phase de transformation, lors de laquelle il a combiné des éléments anciens en pierre et en bois avec des peaux et de la feutrine pour le capitonnage.

The interior reflects the owner's passion for art. The walls exclusively feature the works of notable artists from Switzerland.

Das Interieur spiegelt die Kunstleidenschaft des Besitzers wieder. An den Wänden befinden sich ausschließlich Werke namhafter Künstler aus der Schweiz.

L'intérieur illustre la passion du maître des lieux pour l'art. Les murs accueillent exclusivement des œuvres d'artistes suisses de renom.

Chesa Pichalain

St. Moritz, Switzerland

Originally built in the 1950s, Chesa Pichalain was renovated and refurbished by its current owners. Because the original façade was completely retained, the house feels very traditional from the outside. The interior spaces, however, reveal how Alpine materials can be used to great effect in a modern design scheme. Engadin granite and reclaimed wooden planks were employed for the floors. Aged wood featuring an elegant patina was used for some of the walls and furniture. Loden fabric so characteristic of the mountains has been chosen for cushion covers and drapes. The sparse interior in muted natural hues offers plenty of space for creative design elements. French painter Mathias Kiss painted a mural of the mountains on the walls along the staircase, and a Breton artist made chairs out of Engadin wood.

Die heutigen Eigentümer haben die in den 50er Jahren gebaute Chesa Pichalain renoviert und neu eingerichtet. Von außen wirkt das Haus mit seiner alten, komplett erhaltenen Fassade ganz traditionell. Die Innenräume zeigen hingegen, wie modern man mit den Materialien der Alpenwelt gestalten kann. Auf den Böden sind Engadiner Granit oder Bohlen aus Altholz verlegt. Auch einige der Wände und Möbel wurden aus Holz gefertigt, das durch die Alterung bereits eine elegante Patina zeigt. Für die Bergwelt typisch sind ebenso die Polsterbezüge und Vorhänge aus Loden. Das sparsam gewählte Interieur in gedeckten Naturtönen lässt viel Raum für kreative Gestaltungselemente. So hat der französische Maler Mathias Kiss die Wände entlang der Treppe mit einem Bergmotiv bemalt, und ein bretonischer Künstler fertigte Stühle aus Engadiner Holz an.

Les propriétaires actuels ont rénové et réaménagé la villa Chesa Pichalain, construite dans les années 50. L'ancienne façade extérieure, entièrement conservée, confère à l'édifice un style traditionnel. La décoration des pièces intérieures contraste cependant avec l'ensemble et prouve qu'il est possible d'utiliser des matériaux des Alpes pour un assemblage des plus modernes. Les sols sont recouverts de granit d'Engadine ou de planches de vieux bois. Certains murs et meubles sont également en bois, qui sous l'effet du temps se patinent élégamment. Les revêtements rembourrés et les rideaux en loden sont typiques du décor montagnard. L'intérieur modeste aux teintes naturelles constitue un support idéal pour un aménagement créatif. Le peintre français Mathias Kiss a ainsi laissé libre cours à son imagination en décorant les murs de la cage d'escalier d'un paysage montagnard, et les chaises en bois d'Engadine sont l'œuvre d'un artiste breton.

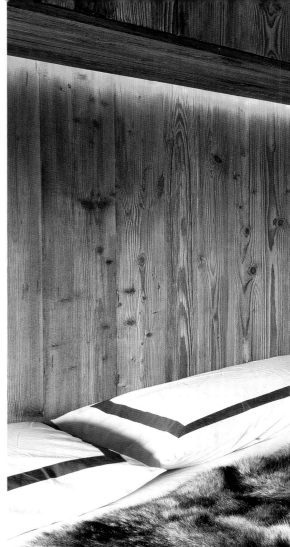

Modern shapes of the fireplace blend harmoniously with individual pieces from gnarled, untreated wood. The indirect lighting at the head of the bed bathes the old Engadin wood in a cozy light.

Moderne Formen am Kamin und Einzelstücke aus naturbelassenem, knorrigem Holz ergänzen sich harmonisch. Die indirekte Beleuchtung am Kopfende des Bettes taucht das alte Engadiner Holz in behagliches Licht.

Les formes modernes de la cheminée s'accordent harmonieusement aux pièces uniques en bois naturel et noueux. L'éclairage indirect de la tête du lit rehausse agréablement le ton du vieux bois d'Engadine.

Der Turm

St. Moritz, Switzerland

The first resident of the tower was famous playboy, philanthropist, art collector, and photographer Gunter Sachs. In 1969 when he moved in, Sachs' new residence with its view of Lake St. Moritz became a Mecca for art lovers. Andy Warhol, Yves Klein, René Magritte, Salvador Dalí and Roy Lichtenstein did more than just decorate Sachs' luxury apartment with their works, they also maintained close contact with the passionate art collector. When Sachs left, Swiss publisher Jürg Marquard took over the single story tower suite and added two additional levels to it. A salon, dining area, and fireplace room occupy the first floor. Three luxuriously appointed bedrooms are located on the second floor. The third story is spectacular: The master bedroom offers a breathtaking 180-degree view of the Engadin valley.

Der erste Bewohner des Turms war der berühmte Playboy, Philanthrop, Kunstsammler und Fotograf Gunter Sachs. Mit seinem Einzug 1969 machte Sachs seinen neuen Wohnsitz mit Sicht über den St. Moritzersee zum Mekka vieler Kunstliebhaber. Andy Warhol, Yves Klein, René Magritte, Salvador Dalí und Roy Lichtenstein schmückten nicht nur mit ihren Werken Sachs' Luxusappartement. Sie pflegten auch regen Kontakt zu dem leidenschaftlichen Kunstsammler. Mit Sachs' Wegzug übernahm der Schweizer Verleger Jürg Marquard die einstöckige Turmsuite und baute sie auf drei Geschosse aus. Das erste Stockwerk besteht aus Salon, Essbereich und Kaminzimmer. Im zweiten Stock befinden sich drei luxuriös ausgestattete Schlafzimmer. Spektakulär ist die dritte Etage: Der Masterbedroom bietet eine atemberaubende 180-Grad-Aussicht auf das Engadin.

Le premier propriétaire de cette tour était le célèbre playboy, philanthrope, collectionneur d'art et photographe Gunter Sachs. En emménageant au Turm en 1969, Sachs faisait de son nouveau domicile dominant le lac de Saint-Moritz, une authentique Mecque de l'art pour de nombreux amateurs. Non seulement Andy Warhol, Yves Klein, René Magritte, Salvador Dalí et Roy Lichtenstein rehaussaient la luxueuse résidence de Sachs de leurs œuvres, mais ils entretenaient aussi de véritables relations avec ce collectionneur passionné. Lorsque Sachs quitta les lieux, l'éditeur suisse Jürg Marquard reprit la suite et l'agrandit sur trois niveaux. Le premier comporte un séjour, une salle à manger et un salon avec cheminée. Le deuxième accueille trois chambres luxueuses et le troisième est spectaculaire : la chambre principale offre un panorama époustouflant sur l'Engadine.

Jürg Marquard and his patchwork family cherish the three-story tower suite as a place to relax. At the same time, the bright, open-plan living rooms provide an ideal setting for the elaborate dinner parties that the publisher and his wife, Raquel, like to throw.

Jürg Marquard und seine Patchworkfamilie schätzen die dreistöckige Turmsuite als Ort der Entspannung. Gleichzeitig sind die hell und offen gestalteten Wohnräume der ideale Rahmen für Feste, die der Verleger und seine Gattin Raquel gerne ausrichten.

Jürg Marquard et sa famille recomposée goûtent tout particulièrement la détente qu'offre cette suite en triplex. D'un autre côté, les espaces ouverts des pièces à vivre très lumineuses constituent le cadre idéal pour les fêtes que l'éditeur et son épouse organisent avec plaisir.

La Quinta

St. Moritz, Switzerland

When the current owners bought La Quinta, built in 1967, they wanted to express their individual style during the renovation. Since the building had already had two interesting owners, they also wanted to retain elements of the past. As a result, the owners kept the layout of the rooms and some of the furniture and chose to go with a timelessly classical style for the furnishings. They didn't want anything to disrupt the harmony between the interior spaces and the incredibly beautiful views. The pool in the basement is a new addition. A friend of the owners, artist Robert Bazelaire, and architect Jean de Ponfilly designed the cavernous wellness area. Depending on how they look at it, guests can interpret the artistic wall installation as flying stones or as clouds fallen from the sky.

Als die jetzigen Bewohner das 1967 erbaute Haus La Quinta übernommen haben, wollten sie bei der Renovierung ihren eigenen Stil verwirklichen. Da das Gebäude bereits zwei interessante Vorbesitzer hatte, sollte aber auch die Vergangenheit weiterhin sichtbar bleiben. Die Eigentümer übernahmen deshalb die Raumaufteilung und einige Möbel. Bei der Einrichtung wählten sie einen zeitlos klassischen Stil. Nichts sollte die Harmonie zwischen den Innenräumen und den unglaublich schönen Ausblicken stören. Neu hinzugekommen ist der Pool im Keller. Verantwortlich für die Gestaltung des höhlenartigen Wellnessareals waren der befreundete Künstler Robert Bazelaire und der Architekt Jean de Ponfilly. Die künstlerische Wandgestaltung kann man je nach Lesart als fliegende Steine oder vom Himmel gefallene Wolken deuten.

En acquérant cette maison, érigée en 1967, ses occupants actuels souhaitaient la rénover en fonction de leur goût. Toutefois, étant donné que La Quinta avait déjà connu deux propriétaires dont les travaux d'aménagement avaient produit des espaces intéressants, les nouveaux venus voulaient que cet héritage reste perceptible. C'est la raison pour laquelle ils ont conservé la répartition des pièces, ainsi que quelques éléments de mobilier. En matière de décoration, ils ont opté pour un style classique et intemporel. Rien ne devait rompre l'harmonie entre les espaces intérieurs et la vue incroyable. Au sous-sol, une piscine a été ajoutée. L'artiste Robert Bazelaire, un ami des maîtres des lieux, et l'architecte Jean de Ponfilly ont été chargés d'aménager l'espace bien-être à la manière d'une grotte. La décoration du mur peut être interprétée, en fonction du mode de lecture, soit comme des pierres volantes, soit comme des nuages tombés du ciel.

The furnishings and decorative objects come from mountainous regions
all over the world, which the owners have visited on their many trips.

Die Einrichtungsgegenstände und Deko-Objekte stammen aus Bergregionen
der ganzen Welt, die die Bewohner auf ihren vielen Reisen besucht haben.

Les éléments de décoration et autres accessoires ont été ramenés de diverses régions
montagneuses que les propriétaires ont visitées lors de leurs voyages dans le monde entier.

Olympiastadion

St. Moritz, Switzerland

Built for the 1928 Olympic Winter Games and then used again for the 1948 Olympics, this Bauhaus structure was designed by Swiss architect Valentin Koch and served as a spectator stand and referee center. The current owner and furniture designer Rolf Sachs moved in together with his artwork in 2006. The restoration used materials typical for the area, such as larch and Swiss stone pine or Andeer and gray granite. White or red-painted walls form the ideal backdrop for paintings from the Russian avant-garde movement and Graubünden antiques. The furnishings reflect the time in which the structure was built and include pieces from the Bauhaus, De Stijl, and the Wiener Werkstätte movements as well as a collection from Gerrit Rietvelt. These classics blend harmoniously with contemporary designs from Marc Newson, Maarten Baas, and Rolf Sachs himself.

Das Haus wurde anlässlich der Olympischen Winterspiele 1928 erbaut und auch für die Spiele 1948 genutzt. Konzipiert vom Schweizer Architekten Valentin Koch im damals zeitgemäßen Bauhausstil, diente es als Zuschauerstand und Schiedsrichter-Zentrum. 2006 zog der heutige Besitzer, Möbeldesigner Rolf Sachs, ein – und mit ihm die Kunst. Bei der Restauration des Baudenkmals wurden ortstypische Materialien verwendet wie Lärchen- oder Arvenholz und Andeerer oder grauer Granit. Die weiß verputzten oder roten Wände sind ein idealer Hintergrund für Bilder der russischen Avantgarde und Bündner Antiquitäten. Die Einrichtung orientiert sich an der Entstehungszeit des Gebäudes und umfasst Möbel vom Bauhaus, De Stijl, der Wiener Werkstätte sowie eine Sammlung von Gerrit Rietvelt. Die Klassiker harmonieren mit zeitgenössischen Entwürfen von Marc Newson, Maarten Baas und Rolf Sachs selbst.

Construit pour les Jeux olympiques d'hiver de 1928, puis utilisé lors des Jeux de 1948, cet édifice Bauhaus a été conçu par l'architecte suisse Valentin Koch. Il servait de plateforme d'observation et de centre d'arbitrage. En 2006 le designer Rolf Sachs l'a acquis. Lors de la restauration, on a recouru aux matériaux de la région, tels que le bois de mélèze ou d'arole, ou le granit Andeer et le granit gris. Les murs blancs et rouges constituent le support idéal pour les tableaux de l'avant-garde russe ou les antiquités de la région des Grisons. La décoration, en phase avec la période de construction du bâtiment, comporte des meubles de style Bauhaus, De Stijl et Wiener Werkstätte, ainsi qu'une collection de Gerrit Rietvelt. Ces classiques cohabitent avec des créations contemporaines de Marc Newson, de Maarten Baas et de Rolf Sachs lui-même.

Residenzia Rosatsch

St. Moritz, Switzerland

The owners of Residenzia Rosatsch, conceptualized by Hans-Jörg Ruch, have been fans of French interior designer Patrice Nourissat for years, so it comes as no surprise that Nourissat was responsible for the furnishing. The site's breathtaking view of Lake St. Moritz was the most important source of inspiration for the owners. The designers of the house deliberately chose simple and clear shapes to facilitate the dialog between architecture, interior design, and the uniquely beautiful landscape. Contrasts in black and white dominate the color palette. The most beautiful area in the house is the open and spacious living room. Accessible from two sides, the fireplace divides the space into living and dining areas. From the expansive sofa with numerous comfortable cushions, guests can relax and enjoy the fantastic natural panoramas.

Verantwortlich für die Konzipierung des Hauses ist der Architekt Hans-Jörg Ruch. Die Einrichtung übernahm der französische Dekorateur Patrice Nourissat, dessen Arbeit die Besitzer seit vielen Jahren schätzen. Die wichtigste Inspirationsquelle für den Bauherrn war der atemberaubende Blick auf den St. Moritzersee, den das Grundstück bietet. Die Gestalter des Hauses wählten bewusst einfache und klare Formen, damit Architektur und Inneneinrichtung mit der einzigartig schönen Landschaft in Dialog treten können. Bei den Farben dominieren Kontraste in Schwarz und Weiß. Der schönste Platz des Hauses ist das offen gestaltete, großzügige Wohnzimmer. Der von zwei Seiten zugängliche Kamin teilt den Raum in Wohn- und Essbereich. Von der mit vielen gemütlichen Kissen bestückten Sofalandschaft aus kann der Bewohner die fantastischen Naturpanoramen entspannt genießen.

La conception de la Residenzia Rosatsch a été confié à l'architecte Hans-Jörg Ruch, la décoration au français Patrice Nourissat, un professionnel dont les propriétaires apprécient le travail depuis de nombreuses années. Le maître des lieux a été principalement inspiré par la vue sur le lac de Saint-Moritz, à couper le souffle. Les créateurs de la maison ont choisi des formes simples et pures, afin que l'architecture et la décoration soient en parfaite harmonie avec la beauté exceptionnelle du paysage. En termes de couleur, les contrastes noir et blanc sont omniprésents. La plus belle pièce de la maison est la vaste salle de séjour aménagée en espace ouvert. La cheminée, accessible de deux côtés, sépare les fonctions : d'un côté le salon et de l'autre la salle à manger. Confortablement installés sur les coussins douillets des canapés, les occupants peuvent se détendre en contemplant ce fantastique panorama sur la nature.

The dining area features a dark solid wood table surrounded by chairs by Mart Stam, the inventor of the cantilever chair. The living room is decorated with abstract paintings and modern sculptures.

Im Essbereich steht ein Tisch aus dunklem Massivholz, umgeben von Stühlen von Mart Stam, dem Erfinder des Freischwingers. Das Wohnzimmer ist mit abstrakter Malerei und modernen Skulpturen dekoriert.

Dans la salle à manger, on trouve une table en bois sombre massif, entourée de chaises signées Mart Stam, l'inventeur de la chaise cantilever. Le séjour est rehaussé de peintures abstraites et de sculptures modernes.

La Stailina

Suvretta, Switzerland

Built in 1959, La Stailina was one of the first houses to be constructed on the mountain plateau near Suvretta; today, the property features one of the best locations in the region. The current owner worked with architect Martin Fischer to remodel the building. The interior furnishings by Axel Vervoordt reflect the Japanese aesthetic of wabi-sabi. According to this philosophy, beauty is found in close proximity to nature and is a state characterized by imperfection. To elicit the natural poetry of objects, the interior of La Stailina has a very restrained color palette, with dominant tones of gray and anthracite. The interior designers selectively set accents using modern art, sophisticated materials such as fur, and avant-garde lighting objects. The interior shows just how luxurious a simple and restrained style can feel.

La Stailina gehört zu den ersten Häusern, die im Jahr 1959 auf dem Plateau der Berge um Suvretta errichtet wurden. Deshalb steht das Anwesen heute in einer der besten Lagen der Region. Der jetzige Besitzer hat das Gebäude in Zusammenarbeit mit dem Architekten Martin Fischer neu gestaltet. Die Inneneinrichtung, erstellt von Axel Vervoordt, orientiert sich am Geist der japanischen Wabi-Sabi-Ästhetik. Nach diesem Konzept ist Schönheit ein unperfekter, möglichst naturnaher Zustand. Der Gestalter möchte den Dingen ihre ureigene Poesie entlocken. Das Interieur des Hauses La Stailina ist deshalb bei der Farbwahl sehr zurückhaltend: Es dominieren Grau- und Anthrazittöne. Mit moderner Kunst, edlen Materialien wie Pelz sowie avantgardistischen Lichtobjekten setzen die Einrichter gezielt Akzente. Das Interieur zeigt, wie luxuriös ein schlichter, reduzierter Stil wirken kann.

La Stailina compte parmi les premières maisons construites en 1959 sur le plateau autour de Suvretta, raison pour laquelle elle jouit de l'un des meilleurs emplacements de la région. Le propriétaire actuel a réaménagé le bâtiment en collaboration avec l'architecte Martin Fischer, s'inspirant pour la décoration de l'esthétique japonaise wabi-sabi. Selon ce concept, la beauté correspond à un état imparfait aussi proche que possible de la nature. Le décorateur a souhaité révéler la poésie authentique et caractéristique des choses. Le choix des coloris à l'intérieur de La Stailina s'illustre par sa sobriété, avec une dominance des tons gris et anthracite. Le mobilier a été conçu par Axel Vervoordt. Par ailleurs, les décorateurs ont délibérément choisi des œuvres d'art contemporain, des matériaux nobles comme la peau, ainsi que des luminaires avant-gardistes. Tous ces aménagements illustrent à quel point un style simple et épuré peut être luxueux.

The planks of the dining room table have been left in their natural state, reflecting the aesthetic of wabi-sabi. Madelaine Lys created the lighting sculpture. The ironwork on the fireplace and on the staircase by Enrico Giacometti provide this authentic mountain style a breath of modernism.

Die Bohlen des Esstisches sind ganz im Geiste des Wabi-Sabi naturbelassen. Die Leuchtskulptur darüber ist ein Werk von Madelaine Lys. Die Eisenarbeiten am Kamin und der Treppe von Enrico Giacometti geben dieser authentischen Bergwelt eine Brise robuste Modernität.

Les planches de la table, en bois brut, relèvent de l'esprit wabi-sabi. Madelaine Lys a créé la sculpture lumineuse au-dessus de la table. Les ferronneries de la cheminée et de l'escalier signées Enrico Giacometti apportent à cet authentique chalet une touche résolument contemporaine.

Hidden Dragon

Valais, Switzerland

With the construction of Hidden Dragon, a 7,500-square-foot chalet located at an elevation of 5,000 feet in the Valais Alps, Ashlee Benis and her brother Andre fulfilled a dream. Shortly before construction began, they were contacted by their Japanese grandmother. The elderly lady insisted that they include a Shinto priest in the planning of the project. In Shintoism, people believe that all earthly things are inhabited by gods. To appease the gods, the siblings first scattered pounds of salt on the property. Afterwards, they soothed the gods with rice, water, and the fragrance of incense sticks. What emerged is a magical place charged with energy and architectural elements with a hint of an Asian influence. If you visit this chalet, you should definitely plan on packing your yoga mat because the owners offer yoga, reiki, and tai chi courses with a view of the majestic Alpine peaks.

Ashlee Benis und ihr Bruder Andre haben sich mit dem Bau des 700 Quadratmeter großen Chalets Hidden Dragon auf 1 500 Metern Höhe in den Walliser Alpen einen Traum erfüllt. Kurz vor Baubeginn meldete sich die japanische Großmutter. Die alte Dame drängte darauf, unbedingt einen Shinto-Priester bei dem Projekt hinzuzuziehen. Im Shintoismus glaubt man, alle irdischen Dinge seien von Göttern bewohnt. Um diese gnädig zu stimmen, haben die Geschwister zunächst kiloweise Salz auf dem Grundstück verstreut. Danach besänftigten sie die Götter mit Reis, Wasser und dem Duft von Räucherstäbchen. Entstanden ist ein magischer Ort voller Energie und asiatisch angehauchter Architekturelemente. Kommt man hierher, sollte man unbedingt die Yogamatte mit im Gepäck haben, denn die Besitzer bieten im Angesicht der majestätisch in sich ruhenden Alpengipfel Yoga-, Reiki- oder Tai-Chi-Kurse an.

Ashlee Benis et son frère Andre ont réalisé leur rêve en construisant ce chalet de 700 mètres carrés, nommé Hidden Dragon, à 1 500 mètres d'altitude dans les Alpes Valaisannes. Peu de temps avant le début des travaux, leur grand-mère japonaise les avait contactés. La vieille dame avait insisté pour qu'ils fassent appel à un prêtre shinto pour leur projet. Dans le shintoïsme, toute chose sur terre est habitée par les dieux. Pour obtenir la grâce de ces derniers, le frère et la sœur ont répandu quelques kilos de sel sur le terrain. Ils les ont ensuite apaisés avec du riz, de l'eau et des bâtonnets d'encens. Le résultat est un lieu magique chargé d'énergie et riche en éléments architecturaux aux accents asiatiques. Il est conseillé aux visiteurs qui s'y rendent de mettre leur tapis de yoga dans leur valise. En effet, les propriétaires proposent des cours de yoga, de reiki et de tai-chi avec pour décor les sommets alpins dont la seule majesté a déjà des vertus apaisantes.

Chalet in Verbier

Verbier, Switzerland

The owner of this chalet in Verbier is an enthusiast of Asian art. Tamara's Design from Rougemont was responsible for the chalet's interior design and inserted the collector's items very carefully. They took care not to overload the rooms; instead, they chose a selection of the valuable objects to include in the decor. Federica and Tamara Sessa also exercised restraint when it came to the color palette. Grayish-brown tones and dark anthracite dominate the interior, and the shapes are sleek. This functional and peaceful interior design successfully contrasts with the lively structure of the wood covering the walls and ceilings. The heavily grained beams and boards are dotted with knotholes. In the midst of the wild mountainous surroundings, the Sessas have successfully created a place full of harmony and straightforward beauty.

Der Besitzer des Chalets in Verbier ist ein Liebhaber asiatischer Kunst. Die Inneneinrichter der Hütte, Tamara's Design aus Rougemont, gingen mit den Sammlerstücken sehr behutsam um. Sie überfrachteten die Räume nicht, sondern dekorierten sparsam mit einer gezielten Auswahl wertvoller Objekte. Auch bei den Farben übten die Innenarchitektinnen, Federica und Tamara Sessa, Zurückhaltung. Es dominieren warme Grautöne und dunkles Anthrazit, die Formen sind schlicht. Diese sachliche, ruhige Art des Interieurs stellt einen gelungenen Kontrast dar zu der lebendigen Struktur des Holzes an Decken und Wänden. Inmitten der wilden Bergnatur schafften die Innenarchitektinnen einen Ort voller Harmonie und geradliniger Schönheit.

Le propriétaire du chalet à Verbier est un amateur d'art asiatique, dont les œuvres ont été insérées avec soin par les architectes d'intérieur de Tamara's Design à Rougemont. Sans surcharger les espaces, ces dernières ont sélectionné quelques objets de grande valeur pour les intégrer avec parcimonie à la décoration. De même, Federica et Tamara Sessa, ont fait preuve de discrétion en utilisant une dominance de tons taupe et mastic. Cette vision calme et sobre d'un intérieur aux formes pures contraste brillamment avec les murs et les plafonds en vieux bois, avec ses larges nervures et ses nœuds visibles sur les poutres et les lambris. Les architectes d'intérieur ont réalisé, au cœur du Valais, un endroit parfaitement harmonieux dont les lignes droites renforcent la beauté du lieu.

Tamara's Design conceived the buffet and the two matching coffee tables. In the bedroom, furs create a warm and comfortable atmosphere.

Das Buffet und die beiden korrespondierenden Couchtische hat Tamara's Design entworfen. Im Schlafzimmer sorgt der edle Pelz für eine warme und behagliche Atmosphäre.

Le buffet et les deux tables gigognes sont des créations de Tamara's Design. Dans la chambre, la magnifique fourrure procure une ambiance de chaleur et de bien-être.

The Lodge

Verbier, Switzerland

The Lodge is a stately property located in the heart of the Verbier ski area and belongs to the business empire of British entrepreneur Richard Branson. This mountain chalet has a total of nine bedrooms and can accommodate 18 adults. A bunk room equipped with bunk beds provides accommodation for six additional children or adolescents. Bright natural hues in the interior, the elegant gray-brown of the exposed beams and wooden walls, as well as occasional pops of bright color accents create a comfortable and modern atmosphere. In the winter, the house is the ideal starting point for extensive ski adventures, while daring sports such as canyoning and paragliding beckon in the summer. Afterwards guests can relax and enjoy one of the numerous treatments offered in the chalet's own spa or indulge in international and Swiss cuisine in the dining area.

Das imposante Anwesen The Lodge befindet sich inmitten des Skigebiets von Verbier und gehört zum Imperium des britischen Unternehmers Richard Branson. Das Bergchalet verfügt insgesamt über neun Schlafzimmer für 18 Erwachsene. Sechs weitere Kinder oder Jugendliche finden Platz in einem Raum, der mit Etagenbetten ausgestattet ist. Helle Naturtöne beim Interieur, das elegante Graubraun der freiliegenden Balken und Holzwände sowie vereinzelte Akzente in Knallfarben schaffen eine behagliche und moderne Wohnatmosphäre. Im Winter ist das Haus der ideale Ausgangspunkt für ausgiebige Pistenabenteuer, im Sommer locken waghalsige Sportarten wie Canyoning oder Paragliding. Anschließend entspannt man bei einer der zahlreichen Anwendungen im hauseigenen Spa oder genießt im Speisesaal internationale und Schweizer Küche.

L'impressionnant bâtiment The Lodge situé au cœur de la station de ski de Verbier fait partie de l'empire de l'entrepreneur britannique Richard Branson. Ce chalet de montagne qui dispose de neuf chambres à coucher peut accueillir au total 18 adultes. De plus, six enfants ou adolescents peuvent s'installer dans une chambre aménagée avec des lits superposés. L'intérieur réserve une ambiance moderne et apaisante, grâce à l'utilisation de tons clairs et naturels associés à l'élégance du gris-taupe des poutres apparentes et des lambris, que rehaussent les touches de couleurs vives présentes ici et là. En hiver, la maison est le camp de base idéal pour partir à la découverte de la station, et en été, pour pratiquer les sports casse-cou que sont le canyoning et le parapente. La journée se termine par un moment de détente au spa du Lodge ou à la salle à manger pour déguster des plats suisses ou d'inspiration plus internationale.

Zermatt Peak

Zermatt, Switzerland

Zermatt Peak is a five star boutique chalet located at an elevation of 5,300 feet. Conceived by designer and developer Paul Bowyer, the property is one of the most exclusive chalets in the Alps. Even the location is unique: Guests have an unobstructed view of the majestic Matterhorn. At night, they can enjoy fantastic views of the twinkling lights of Zermatt. In the furnishings, luxury is on display right down to the smallest detail. The light fixtures are made of Murano glass. For the floor finishes, the interior designers chose walnut, Italian marble, and natural stone from Brazil. The upholstered furniture from de Sede is adjustable, allowing guests to comfortably change their view. Bioethanol fire features recessed in the tables create a magical atmosphere in the evenings.

Auf 1 620 Metern über dem Meeresspiegel liegt das Fünf-Sterne-Boutique-Chalet Zermatt Peak. Das von dem Designer und Entwickler Paul Bowyer konzipierte Anwesen gehört zu den exklusivsten Chalets der Alpen. Schon die Lage ist einzigartig: Die Bewohner haben freie Sicht auf das majestätische Bergmassiv des Matterhorns. Nachts genießt man einen fantastischen Blick über die funkelnden Lichter von Zermatt. Bei der Ausstattung herrscht Luxus bis ins kleinste Detail. Die Leuchten sind aus Muranoglas gefertigt. Auf den Böden haben die Einrichter Nussbaum, italienischen Marmor und Naturstein aus Brasilien verlegt. Die Polstermöbel von de Sede sind verstellbar, damit der Bewohner bequem seine Blickrichtung verändern kann. Für eine zauberhafte Stimmung am Abend sorgen in die Tische eingelassene Bioethanol-Feuer.

Le Zermatt Peak, hôtel-boutique cinq étoiles situé à plus de 1 620 mètres au-dessus du niveau de la mer et conçu par le designer Paul Bowyer, compte parmi les chalets les plus sélect des Alpes. Sa situation est unique : les occupants ont une vue dégagée sur le majestueux massif du Matterhorn. La nuit aussi, la vue sur la ville de Zermatt, qui brille de mille feux, est merveilleuse. En matière de décoration, le maître mot est le luxe, jusque dans les moindres détails. Les luminaires sont en verre de Murano. Pour les sols, les décorateurs ont opté pour du noyer, du marbre italien et de la pierre naturelle du Brésil. Les canapés signés de Sede sont mobiles afin d'offrir aux occupants la possibilité de modifier facilement leur angle de vue. Les foyers ouverts, fonctionnant au bioéthanol et intégrés directement dans les tables, garantissent des soirées magiques.

Belmont

Whistler, British Columbia, Canada

Constructed in 2007, the Belmont is one of the largest and most luxurious private properties in the region. Skiers set out by helicopter from the chalet's own helipad for spectacular trips to the glaciers of Whistler Mountain or Blackcomb Peak. The complex includes a main house with five bedrooms, each with its own private bath. The architecture and furnishings are harmoniously coordinated and feel sleek and modern. Just 160 feet away is the guest house featuring two bedrooms and a loft with a living room and kitchen. Amenities at the Belmont also include a heated outdoor pool, sauna, steam bath, and fitness room. On summer evenings, the fire pit on the terrace with its elegant lounge furniture is the perfect place to bring the day to a close while taking in panoramic mountain views.

Das im Jahr 2007 gebaute Belmont gehört zu den größten und luxuriösesten privaten Anwesen der Region. Skifahrer brechen per Helikopter vom hauseigenen Landeplatz auf zu spektakulären Trips auf den Gletschern von Whistler Mountain oder Blackcomb Peak. Zu dem Komplex gehört ein Haupthaus mit fünf Schlafzimmern, jedes mit eigenem Bad ausgestattet. Architektur und Einrichtung sind harmonisch aufeinander abgestimmt und wirken geradlinig und modern. 50 Meter entfernt befindet sich das Gästehaus mit zwei Schlafzimmern sowie einem Loft zum Wohnen und Kochen. Zur Ausstattung des Belmont gehören außerdem ein beheizter Freiluftpool, Sauna, Dampfbad und Fitnessraum. An Sommerabenden ist die Feuerstelle auf der Terrasse mit ihren eleganten Loungemöbeln der ideale Ort, um mit Blick auf das Bergpanorama den Tag ausklingen zu lassen.

Construit en 2007, le Belmont compte parmi les propriétés privées les plus vastes et les plus luxueuses de la région. Les hélicoptères décollent du domaine pour emmener les skieurs sur les glaciers spectaculaires de Whistler Mountain ou Blackcomb Peak. Le bâtiment principal du complexe comporte cinq chambres avec salles de bain. L'architecture et la décoration sont en parfaite harmonie, toutes deux jouant sur un style contemporain et la rectitude des lignes. La maison d'hôte, située 50 mètres plus loin, compte deux chambres ainsi qu'un espace ouvert réunissant séjour et cuisine. Le Belmont est également équipé d'une piscine extérieure chauffée, d'un sauna, d'un hammam et d'une salle de sport. Les soirs d'été, l'élégante terrasse, avec son foyer ouvert et son confortable salon d'extérieur, est le lieu idéal pour profiter du beau panorama qu'offrent les montagnes au crépuscule.

Large windows offering views of the Canadian forest as well as natural stone veneers give the living area a naturalistic ambience.

Große Fensterfronten mit Blick auf den kanadischen Nadelwald sowie Verkleidungen aus Naturstein geben dem Wohnbereich eine äußerst naturverbundene Atmosphäre.

Les grandes baies vitrées qui donnent sur la forêt canadienne, ainsi que les revêtements en pierre naturelle, créent dans le séjour une atmosphère de communion avec la nature.

Bighorn

Revelstoke, British Columbia, Canada

Newly opened for the 2011–12 season, Bighorn is a mountain lodge located in a forested area at the foot of the Revelstoke mountains. From the terrace, guests can enjoy magnificent views of the nearby Columbia River. The house has eight guest rooms, all featuring their own balcony and private bath. Massive arching beams give the entry hall and living room a spacious atmosphere. It is fitting that the head of a Bighorn sheep is mounted above the fireplace; native to this region, its mighty horns do credit to the resort's name. The interior designers chose a color palette featuring vibrant reds as well as textiles with bold plaids. The guest rooms feel less rustic and instead draw upon a clear, modern design language.

Die in der Saison 2011/12 neu eröffnete Berglodge Bighorn liegt inmitten eines Waldgebietes am Fuße des Revelstoke Gebirges. Von der Terrasse aus bieten sich dem Besucher herrliche Blicke auf den nahen Columbia River. Das Haus verfügt über acht Gästezimmer, alle mit eigenem Balkon und privatem Bad. Mächtiges, kuppelartiges Gebälk verleiht Eingangshalle und Wohnzimmer eine großzügige Atmosphäre. Über dem Kamin thront die Büste eines Dickhornschafs, Bighorn im Englischen, das in dieser Region zu Hause ist und mit seinen gewaltigen Hörnern dem Namen des Resorts alle Ehre macht. Bei der Farbgestaltung griffen die Einrichter auf intensive Rottöne sowie Textilien mit kräftigen, karierten Mustern zurück. Die Gästezimmer wirken weniger rustikal und bedienen sich stattdessen einer klareren, modernen Designsprache.

Le chalet de montagne Bighorn, qui a ouvert ses portes lors de la saison 2011/12, est situé en pleine forêt, au pied de la chaîne du mont Revelstoke. La terrasse offre au visiteur de belles vues sur la rivière Columbia toute proche. La maison dispose de huit chambres réservées aux visiteurs, toutes équipées d'un balcon et d'une salle de bain. Le hall d'entrée et le séjour sont empreints d'une atmosphère spacieuse en raison de l'impressionnante charpente voûtée. Sur la cheminée trône la tête d'un mouflon canadien (bighorn en anglais), un animal de la région aux cornes impressionnantes, qui a prêté son nom au complexe. Les décorateurs ont choisi des tons rouges intenses, ainsi que des textiles à grands carreaux. Loin d'être rustique, le style des chambres est simple et contemporain.

Pioneer Springs

Aspen, Colorado, USA

Pioneer Springs is located only minutes away from the lifts that carry skiers high into the snow-covered mountains above Aspen. The owner built this property in 2004 with great attention to detail. At just over 13,000 square feet, the amenities at Pioneer Springs include one master suite, one guest master suite, and five other bedrooms. The outdoor areas are terraced, enabling guests to relax outside on comfortable lounge furniture in front of an architectural backdrop with Mediterranean features. Inside, the atmosphere is luxurious. The open fireplace with its minimalist design is an impressive piece of modern architecture. With its cooking island, the kitchen offers plenty of space and state-of-the-art technology. Translucent cabinet fronts contribute to the airy impression of the entire room.

Pioneer Springs befindet sich nur wenige Minuten entfernt von den Lifts, die die Skifahrer hoch in die schneebedeckten Berge Aspens bringen. Der Besitzer hat das Anwesen 2004 mit viel Liebe zum Detail erbaut. Auf insgesamt 1 200 Quadratmetern Wohnfläche sind unter anderem fünf konventionelle Schlafzimmer, eine Gästesuite sowie eine Mastersuite untergebracht. Die Außenflächen wurden treppenförmig, auf unterschiedlichen Ebenen angelegt. Man entspannt im Freien auf bequemen Loungemöbeln vor einer architektonischen Kulisse, die mediterrane Züge trägt. Das Ambiente im Inneren ist luxuriös. Ein beeindruckendes Stück moderner Architektur ist der minimalistisch gestaltete, offene Kamin. Die Küche bietet mit ihrer Kochinsel viel Platz und neueste Technik. Halbdurchsichtige Schrankfronten unterstützen den luftigen Eindruck des gesamten Raumes.

Construite en 2004 dans l'amour du détail par son propriétaire actuel, la villa Pioneer Springs se situe à quelques minutes des remontées mécaniques qui emmènent les skieurs sur les sommets enneigés des montagnes d'Aspen. Elle totalise 1 200 mètres carrés de surface habitable et compte cinq chambres, une suite d'hôtes et une suite de maître. Sur les espaces extérieurs aménagés en gradins, on profite du bon air pour se détendre dans de confortables canapés, au milieu de ce décor architectonique aux accents méditerranéens. L'ambiance à l'intérieur est fastueuse. Le foyer ouvert, aussi impressionnant que minimaliste, est une merveille d'architecture contemporaine. La vaste cuisine dispose d'un îlot central et d'appareils électroménagers dernier cri. L'impression de légèreté qui s'en dégage est soulignée par des portes de placards en verre semi-transparent.

Guests do not need to cook themselves: If they prefer, they can
let themselves be pampered by a butler and a private chef.

Selbst Kochen muss der Gast hier nicht. Wer an dieser Tafel Platz nimmt, kann
sich auf Wunsch von einem Butler und einem privaten Koch verwöhnen lassen.

Ici, la cuisine n'est pas une contrainte. S'il le souhaite, le client peut
s'en remettre à un majordome ou un cuisinier qui saura le combler.

Chalet Antonia

Aspen, Colorado, USA

Chalet Antonia in the American ski area of Aspen is luxuriously furnished without losing any of its authentic chalet charm. In 5,700 square feet of space, this home offers five bedrooms, six baths, a living room, dining room, billiards room, and an office. Floor-to-ceiling windows connect the living space to the picturesque scenery of Aspen. The kitchen and a fireplace made of natural stone are located on the lower level. Comfortable upholstered furniture and a blazing fire form a cozy contrast to the rugged Rocky Mountains. The bedrooms are located on the upper level. Crafted out of massive branches, four-poster beds exude the energy of the surrounding forests. Traditional quilts underscore the homey look.

Das in der Wintersportregion Aspen errichtete Chalet ist luxuriös ausgestattet, verzichtet dabei aber nicht auf einen authentischen Hütten-charme. Das Gebäude bietet auf 530 Quadratmetern Wohnfläche fünf Schlafzimmer, sechs Bäder, Wohn- und Esszimmer sowie Billardraum und Büro. Große, vollverglaste Fensterfronten lassen das Ambiente des Wohnraums als Teil der malerischen Landschaft Aspens erscheinen. Im unteren Stockwerk befinden sich die Küche und der aus Natursteinen gemauerte Kamin. Komfortable Polstermöbel und lodernde Flammen bilden einen heimeligen Gegenpol zur schroffen Natur der Rocky Mountains. Im oberen Stockwerk sind die Schlafzimmer untergebracht. Die aus massiven Ästen gezimmerten Himmelbetten verströmen die Energie der umgebenden Wälder. Traditionelle Quilts unterstreichen den heimatverbundenen Look.

Ce Chalet, situé près d'Aspen, haut lieu des sports d'hiver américains, est aménagé avec luxe mais arbore un charme montagnard authen-tique. Sur 530 mètres carrés de surface habitable, il dispose de cinq chambres à coucher, de six salles de bain et d'un séjour-salle à manger, ainsi que d'une salle de billard et d'un bureau. Grâce à de larges baies vitrées le séjour semble se fondre dans le paysage pittoresque d'Aspen. L'étage inférieur accueille la cuisine ainsi que la cheminée en pierre naturelle. La nature sauvage des montagnes Rocheuses contraste avec le spectacle des flammes et les canapés douillets qui invitent au cocooning. Dans les chambres de l'étage, les branches qui constituent la structure des lits à baldaquin restituent l'énergie des forêts environnantes, tandis que les courtepointes traditionnelles rappellent la douceur d'une maison familiale.

*In the open kitchen, wooden cabinets blend with granite countertops while
a wrought-iron chandelier and a metal stove create a rustic charm.*

*Holzfronten, Arbeitsflächen aus Granit, ein schmiedeeiserner Leuchter
und der Metallherd versprühen in der offenen Küche rustikalen Charme.*

*Les portes des placards en bois, les plans de travail en granit, le lustre en fer forgé
et le piano métallique confèrent à cette cuisine ouverte un certain charme rustique.*

Mountain Star Residence

Avon, Colorado, USA

A synergy of old world stone, richly patinated copper siding, refined steel railings, exposed steel and wood structure, and expansive window walls coalesce into a casually elegant modern mountain retreat. While the material palette blends the residence into the surroundings, much of the architectural design was developed to provide a dynamic showcase for the owners' extensive art collection. This requirement of large areas of uninterrupted walls leads to the loftlike entry with the striking gallery space. The kitchen, living room, and outdoor living spaces are focused around the pool and feature spectacular mountain views. The interior is characterized by bright hues, primarily gray and white. Refined steel detailing throughout the house provides a sophisticated edge to the natural materials and traditional roof elements.

Traditionelles Mauerwerk, patinierte Kupferverkleidung, hochwertige Stahlgeländer, freiliegende Stahl- und Holzelemente sowie groß-züge Glasfronten bilden eine Synergie aus lässiger Eleganz und modernem Bergambiente. Während der Materialmix das Anwesen wunderbar in die Landschaft einbettet, wurde architektonisch ein geschicktes Konzept geschaffen, um die große Kunstsammlung der Besitzer zu präsentieren. Lange, ununterbrochene Wände führen zu einem loftähnlichen Eingangsbereich mit beeindruckender Galerie. Die Küche, der Wohnraum und die Außenanlage umgeben den Pool und bieten einen atemberaubenden Blick auf die Berge. Helle Töne, vorwiegend Grau und Weiß, sowie Stahl bestimmen das gesamte Interieur und verleihen den verschiedenen Naturmaterialien und traditionellen Decken-elementen noch mehr Charme.

Le jeu des maçonneries traditionnelles, les revêtements en cuivre patiné, les ferronneries, les charpentes apparentes et les grandes baies vitrées, donne à ce refuge montagnard une allure contemporaine, élégante et simple. Bien que la palette des matériaux lui permette de se fondre dans le décor, le but principal était de libérer de grandes surfaces murales pour exposer la vaste collection d'œuvres d'art du propriétaire. Cette contrainte a donné naissance à l'entrée et à sa remarquable salle d'exposition aux allures de loft. La cuisine, la salle de séjour et les espaces extérieurs s'organisent autour de la piscine et cadrent avec une vue spectaculaire sur les montagnes. Des prédominances de gris et de blanc animent l'intérieur. Dans tout le chalet, la finition des aciers confère aux matériaux naturels et aux éléments traditionnels du toit un caractère sophistiqué.

The kitchen from Bulthaup opens onto the Family room. The Master bedroom on the main level floor offers modern furnishings as well as a high level of comfort. Teak wall panels with aluminum reveals behind the bed add a rich accent.

Die Küche von Bulthaup ist zum Wohnraum hin offen gestaltet. Das große Schlafzimmer im oberen Stockwerk ist modern eingerichtet und bietet ebenso viel Komfort. Die Teakholztäfelung mit Aluminiumrahmen am Kopfende des Bettes setzt einen raffinierten Akzent.

La cuisine Bulthaup s'ouvre sur la salle de séjour. À l'étage principal, la grande chambre est équipée de tout le confort souhaité et d'un mobilier moderne. À la tête du lit, des boiseries en teck avec des encadrements d'aluminium apportent une touche distinguée à l'ensemble.

Rosenbach Residence

Vail, Colorado, USA

The complete renovation of a home built in 1962 resulted in what is now the Rosenbach Residence. K.H. Webb Architects was given the task of rebuilding the house and improving its views of the outdoors while retaining the original character of the structure. During the modernization, the architects were very cautious about employing rustic style elements. All the walls have a smooth plaster finish. Natural stone and exposed stonework are used only sporadically. Local craftsmen custom made all the furniture and built-ins. The architects attached great importance to redesigning the entrance area. The front door crafted out of walnut and Zinc now opens onto an impressive entrance decorated with stylish ceiling lights and wall sconces.

Die heutige Rosenbach Residence ist entstanden durch den Umbau eines 1962 errichteten Wohnhauses. Das Büro K.H. Webb Architects hatte die Aufgabe, das Haus zu modernisieren und die Sicht nach draußen zu verbessern. Dabei sollte der ursprüngliche Charakter des Gebäudes erhalten bleiben. Rustikale Stilelemente setzten die Architekten bei der Modernisierung nur noch sehr zurückhaltend ein. Alle Wände sind glatt verputzt. Nur vereinzelt kommt Naturstein oder sichtbares Mauerwerk zum Einsatz. Sämtliche Möbel und Einbauten haben lokale Handwerker eigens angefertigt. Großen Wert legten die Architekten auf die Neugestaltung des Eingangsbereiches. Hinter der aus Walnussholz und Zink gefertigten Eingangstür öffnet sich jetzt ein imposantes Entree, das mit stilvollen Decken- und Seitenleuchten dekoriert ist.

La Rosenbach Residence est née des transformations d'une maison construite en 1962. Le cabinet K.H. Webb Architects avait été chargé de le moderniser et d'en améliorer les vues, mais sans modifier son caractère original. Les architectes ont donc procédé à l'intégration d'éléments rustiques avec une prudence extrême. Tous les murs ont été recouverts d'un enduit, sauf en de rares endroits où ils ont été laissés à nu, avec parfois de la pierre apparente. L'ensemble des meubles et des installations a été réalisé par des artisans locaux. Les architectes ont donné une grande importance au réaménagement de l'entrée. Désormais, la porte d'entrée, réalisée en bois de noyer et zinc, s'ouvre sur un hall majestueux, rehaussé de plafonniers et d'appliques qui ne manquent pas de style.

Following the renovation, the raised terrace offers improved views of the surrounding landscape.
Suffused with light, the focal point of the bathroom is the spacious shower fully enclosed in glass.

Die erhöhte Terrasse bietet nach dem Umbau eine verbesserte Sicht auf die umgebende Natur.
Das Zentrum des lichtdurchfluteten Badezimmers ist die vollverglaste, geräumige Wellness-Dusche.

Suite à ces transformations, la terrasse surélevée offre une meilleure vue sur la nature environnante. Une
douche bien-être, vaste et entièrement vitrée, est placée au centre de la salle de bain baignée de lumière.

Urban Chalet

Park City, Utah, USA

Principal designer Angela Sarmiento and architect Michael Upwall designed this house in Park City, an exclusive ski area that was once a gold and silver mining town. The owners wanted a property that went beyond the typical chalet clichés. The design team succeeds in this respect due to its size alone: It has eight bedrooms and twelve bathrooms. Guests enter the chalet through a porte cochère steel and wood structure visible from a distance. Inside, huge expanses of windows reveal views of the ski run, surrounding aspens and overlook Park City. The furnishings reflect a classically modern style. The entire lower level is dedicated to entertainment, featuring a bar, billiards table, climbing wall, and an artist's studio with a pottery kiln. A simple railing divides the open upstairs gallery from the lower level so the living room extends two stories to the ceiling.

Designerin Angela Sarmiento und Architekt Michael Upwall gestalteten das Haus im exklusiven Skigebiet Park City, einst eine Bergbaustadt für Gold- und Silbergräber. Die Besitzer wünschten sich ein Anwesen, das über typische Hüttenklischees hinausgehen sollte. Das gelingt dem Urban Chalet schon alleine wegen seiner Größe: Acht Schlafzimmer und zwölf Bäder finden hier Platz. Der Gast betritt das Chalet durch ein von weitem sichtbares Eingangsportal aus Holz und Stahl. Im Inneren geben riesige Fensterflächen den Blick auf die Wälder und Pisten frei. Die Möblierung ist durchweg sehr hochwertig, im klassisch modernen Stil gehalten. Das komplette untere Stockwerk dient der Unterhaltung. Dort befinden sich die Bar, ein Billardtisch, Kletterwand sowie das Künstleratelier mit Brennofen zum Töpfern. Das Obergeschoss öffnet sich mit einem simplen Geländer zum unteren Wohnbereich, sodass die Raumhöhe über zwei Etagen geht.

La designer Angela Sarmiento et l'architecte Michael Upwall sont aménagé ce chalet situé dans la très sélecte station de Park City, célèbre pour ces anciennes mines d'or et d'argent. Les propriétaires souhaitaient éviter le cliché de la cabane de montagne, même si, étant donné que la demeure ne compte pas moins de huit chambres et de douze salles de bain, toute comparaison serait disproportionnée. Le visiteur entre par une porte cochère en bois et acier, visible au loin. Une fois à l'intérieur, les immenses fenêtres offrent une vue dégagée sur la forêt, puis le regard se pose sur un mobilier cossu à la fois contemporain et classique. L'étage inférieur est entièrement consacré au divertissement. On y trouve le bar, un billard, un mur d'escalade ainsi qu'un atelier avec four à poterie. Le palier de l'étage supérieur s'ouvre en mezzanine sur le séjour en double hauteur.

The gas fireplace behind the bar is recessed in the wall. Even the style of furnishings in the bedrooms
is classically modern—only the antlers above the bed reference the traditional chalet style.

Der Gaskamin hinter der Bar ist bündig in die Wand eingelassen. Auch der Einrichtungsstil der
Schlafzimmer ist klassisch modern – nur das Geweih über dem Bett zitiert den traditionellen Hüttenstil.

Derrière le bar, la cheminée au gaz est encastrée dans le mur. Le style des chambres à coucher est
lui aussi à la fois contemporain et classique – seuls les bois de cervidé au-dessus du lit évoquent la
décoration montagnarde typique.

Miyabi and Tsubaki

Niseko, Japan

The region surrounding Niseko in Japan is considered to be one of the most stunning ski areas in the world. Some even refer to the village of Hirafu as the "Aspen of the East." This is the setting for this mountain residence with two identical houses situated next to each other: Miyabi and Tsubaki. The chalets combine the luxury of western comfort with the chic of Japanese finishings. Vaulted ceilings supported by seamless Hokkaido ash posts and beams, an expansive living area, and large windows amplify the 2,700 feet of space. Exemplary timber craftsmanship, ancient wall rendering techniques, a hinoki wood spa, and featured detailing lend the chalet a distinctly Japanese touch. Committed to sustainable building, the design team used local materials whenever possible, including Japanese cedar cladding and Hokkaido oak flooring.

Die Region um Niseko in Japan gilt als eines der schönsten Skigebiete der Welt. Manche nennen das Dorf Hirafu deshalb auch „Aspen des Ostens". Hier liegt die Bergresidenz mit den beiden baugleichen, benachbarten Häusern Miyabi und Tsubaki. Die Chalets kombinieren westlichen Komfort mit eleganter japanischer Wohnkultur. Gewölbte Decken, die von einer raffinierten Holzbalken- und Querträgerkonstruktion aus Eschenholz gestützt werden, der geräumige Wohnbereich sowie große Fenster vergrößern optisch die rund 254 Quadratmeter große Wohnfläche. Schöne Holztäfelungen und traditionelle Verputztechniken an den Wänden schaffen ein edles Ambiente. Der Hinoki-Wellnessbereich verleiht der Residenz ihren besonderen japanischen Charme. Das Designerteam hat — wo immer möglich — nachhaltige Materialien verwendet, unter anderem bei den japanischen Zedernholzverkleidungen und den Hokkaido-Eichenböden.

La région de Niseko, au Japon, est réputée offrir quelques-unes des plus belles stations de ski du monde. Certains appellent même Hirafu « l'Aspen de l'Orient ». C'est ici que se trouve cette résidence de montagne composée de deux bâtiments jumeaux contigus : Miyabi et Tsubaki. Les chalets associent la vision occidentale du confort à l'élégance des finitions japonaises. Les plafonds voûtés supportés par une discrète structure de poutres et de colonnes en frêne d'Hokkaido, le vaste séjour et les larges baies vitrées amplifient la sensation d'espace qu'offre la surface habitable de 254 mètres carrés. Des boiseries remarquables, des murs patinés et un spa en hinoki confèrent au chalet une touche indéniablement japonaise. Engagée en matière de développement durable, l'équipe de construction a fait appel autant que possible à des matériaux locaux comme les revêtements en cèdre du Japon ou le parquet en chêne.

Guests exhausted by a day of skiing can find rejuvenation by soaking in tubs made of Japanese hinoki wood. The extra-deep lounge furniture in front of the fireplace offers another inviting place to relax.

In den Wannen aus japanischem Hinoki-Holz tankt der vom Skifahren erschöpfte Besucher neue Kraft. Auch die extratiefen Loungemöbel vorm Kamin laden zum Entspannen ein.

Les baignoires en hinoki permettent aux skieurs épuisés de se ressourcer et recouvrer leurs forces. Des canapés très profonds placés devant la cheminée invitent à la détente.

Zekkei

Hirafu, Japan

Zekkei extends over three floors and has a total of 4,300 square feet of space. With its open layout and panoramic windows, the spacious living area offers an unobstructed view of a valley with terraced rice fields and impressive Mount Yōtei in the background. Unlike European or American chalets, this chalet does not contain any hunting trophies, animal hides, or other references to the mountains. The typical clichés of Japanese home decor, such as tatami mats or sliding rice paper walls, are absent as well. Instead, the rooms are furnished throughout with modern furniture classics from Europe. Completely liberated from any sort of traditional references, the interior design of this chalet feels very international and timelessly beautiful.

Das Chalet Zekkei erstreckt sich über drei Stockwerke und verfügt über insgesamt 400 Quadratmeter Wohnfläche. Vom großzügigen, offen gestalteten Wohnbereich bieten die Panoramafenster einen unverbauten Blick auf ein Tal mit Reisterrassen und den imposanten Mount Yōtei im Hintergrund. Anders als bei europäischen oder amerikanischen Berghütten findet man in diesem Chalet keine Jagdtrophäen, Tierfelle oder andere Bezüge zur Bergwelt. Auch die typischen Klischees des japanischen Wohnens – Tatamimatten oder Schiebewände aus Reispapier – sucht man in diesem Haus vergebens. Die Räume sind stattdessen durchgängig mit Möbelklassikern der europäischen Moderne ausgestattet. Konsequent befreit von jeder Art von Folklore wirkt der Einrichtungsstil dieses Chalets sehr international und zeitlos schön.

Le chalet Zekkei se déploie sur trois étages, totalisant plus de 400 mètres carrés de surface habitable. Depuis le vaste séjour parfaitement ouvert, les fenêtres panoramiques cadrent des vues sans limites sur la vallée et ses rizières, avec le majestueux mont Yōtei en arrière-plan. Contrairement aux chalets européens ou américains, cette résidence de montagne ne comporte ni trophée de chasse, ni peau, ni aucune autre référence à la culture montagnarde. De même, inutile d'y chercher des clichés de l'habitat japonais traditionnel : pas de tatami ni de cloison coulissante en papier de riz. En effet, le mobilier moderne des pièces reprend exclusivement les classiques du design européen. Ainsi libérée de toute forme de folklore, la décoration très occidentale de cette demeure acquiert une beauté intemporelle.

Classic European pieces dominate the furnishings, including Mies van der Rohe's contribution to the 1929 World Exposition in Barcelona and chairs from legendary Danish designer Hans J. Wegner.

Bei der Möblierung dominieren europäische Designklassiker, darunter Mies van der Rohes Beitrag zur Weltausstellung 1929 in Barcelona oder Stühle des legendären dänischen Designers Hans J. Wegner.

Le mobilier comporte essentiellement des classiques du design européen, dont la contribution de Mies van der Rohe pour l'Exposition internationale de Barcelone de 1929 ou les chaises du designer légendaire danois Hans J. Wegner.

House at the Mountain

Karuizawa, Japan

This house in Karuizawa is a successful example of how modern architecture can also conquer mountains. The structure is unusual for being built on the side of a hill. As a result, guests access the interior rooms by descending rather than ascending the stairs. The fully accessible roof reflects this same architectural style and is also designed like a descending staircase. From this unconventional rooftop terrace, guests can enjoy fantastic views of the treetops. With their simple wood designs, Miurashin Architect + Associates from Tokyo want to convey a clear link to the natural surroundings. They refer to the unusual and highly geometric beam construction as "an abstraction of the forest." The interior is Spartan and takes a back seat to the architecture.

Das Haus in Karuizawa ist ein gelungenes Beispiel dafür, wie moderne Architektur auch die Berge erobert. Das Gebäude ist auf ungewöhnliche Weise an den Hang gebaut. Dementsprechend betritt man die Innenräume, indem man die Eingangstreppe nicht hinauf, sondern hinabsteigt. Das begehbare Dach nimmt diese Bauweise auf und ist ebenfalls in Form einer absteigenden Treppe gestaltet. Von der unkonventionellen Dachterrasse aus genießt der Bewohner fantastische Blicke auf die Baumkronen. Die Architekten, Miurashin Architect + Associates aus Tokyo, möchten mit ihrer schlichten Holzbauweise einen Bezug zur umgebenden Natur herstellen. Die außergewöhnliche, streng geometrische Balkenkonstruktion nennen sie „eine Abstraktion des Waldes". Das Interieur ist spartanisch und ordnet sich der Architektur unter.

Cette maison de Karuizawa est l'exemple d'un mariage réussi entre architecture contemporaine et paysage de montagne. Le bâtiment se répand curieusement dans la pente. Par conséquent, on n'y progresse pas en montant des escaliers, mais en les descendant. Fidèle à cette approche architecturale, le toit en terrasse se répand lui aussi en gradins. De cette terrasse pour le moins non conventionnelle, les occupants profitent d'une vue fantastique sur la cime des arbres. Par la simplicité de ses choix constructifs, le cabinet tokyoïte Miurashin Architect + Associates souhaitait faire référence à la nature environnante. Ils ont appelé cette ossature extraordinaire et strictement géométrique : « abstraction de la forêt ». L'intérieur est spartiate et laisse la vedette à l'architecture.

The architects chose to use larch wood for the walls and cherry and cedar
for the floors. Visitors have to cross a small bridge to reach the entrance.

*Für die Wände verwendeten die Architekten Lärchenholz, am Boden Kirsch-
und Zedernholz. Den Eingang erreicht der Besucher über eine kleine Brücke.*

*Les architectes ont utilisé du bois de mélèze pour les murs, ainsi que du merisier
et du cèdre pour les sols. On accède à l'entrée par une petite passerelle.*

Whare Kea Lodge & Chalet

Wanaka, New Zealand

In the Maori language, "whare kea" means "house of the kea." The kea is the only parrot living above the snow line in the mountains; however, visitors to the Whare Kea Lodge rarely encounter these exotic birds. The guesthouse is located in the snow-free area on the shore of Lake Wanaka, a glacial lake. To spot a kea, visitors have to climb the mountains. The owners expanded the lodge by adding the Whare Kea Chalet at an elevation of 5,700 feet. This modern chalet offers the amenities of a first-class hotel, an unusual feature at this elevation. The chalet can only be reached by helicopter. All building materials had to be transported by helicopter to the site, which quickly ate up one third of the construction costs.

Der Name „Whare Kea" bedeutet in der Sprache der Maori „Haus des Kea". Der Kea ist der einzige Papagei, der oberhalb der Schneegrenze in den Bergen lebt. Auf den exotischen Vogel trifft der Besucher der Whare Kea Lodge allerdings eher selten. Das Gästehaus befindet sich in den noch schneefreien Gebieten, am Ufer des Wanaka-Gletschersees. Um den Kea zu Gesicht zu bekommen, müssen die Besucher hinauf in die Berge. Die Besitzer haben ihre Lodge um das Whare Kea Chalet auf einer Höhe von 1 750 Metern ergänzt. Die moderne Berghütte bietet die Ausstattung eines erstklassigen Hotels, was in dieser Höhe ungewöhnlich ist. Zu erreichen ist das Chalet nur mit dem Helikopter oder zu Fuß. Sämtliche Materialien für den Bau mussten per Helikopter auf die Höhe transportiert werden, was etwa ein Drittel der Baukosten verschlungen hat.

En langue maorie, le nom « Whare Kea » signifie la « maison du kéa ». Le kéa est le seul perroquet vivant en milieu montagnard au-delà de la limite d'enneigement. Néanmoins, le visiteur du Whare Kea Lodge a peu de chances de croiser cet oiseau rare. La maison d'hôte se trouve encore dans le secteur non enneigé au bord du lac glaciaire Wanaka. Pour apercevoir un kéa, les visiteurs doivent grimper plus haut dans les montagnes. Pour ce faire, les propriétaires des lieux ont ajouté à leur offre un chalet moderne, situé à 1 750 mètres d'altitude. Le Whare Kea Chalet offre tout l'équipement d'un hôtel de luxe, ce qui est exceptionnel à cette altitude, et n'est accessible qu'en hélicoptère ou à pied. Tous les matériaux de construction ont dû être héliportés. L'opération a compté pour le tiers du coût du chantier.

Due to the enormous snow loads and wind speeds, steel was used for the
framework of the chalet. In addition, the chalet is constructed on stilts
anchored to boulders to prevent it from sinking into the snow.

Die Rahmenkonstruktion des Chalets ist wegen der enormen Schneelasten und
Windgeschwindigkeiten aus Stahl gefertigt. Zusätzlich steht das Chalet auf
im Geröll verankerten Stelzen, damit es nicht im Schnee versinkt.

La charpente métallique du chalet lui permet de supporter les énormes efforts de
charge de la neige et des vents violents. Le chalet est construit sur des pilotis
solidement ancrés dans la moraine afin de ne pas disparaître dans la neige.

Index

Bärenhütte
Kitzbühel, Austria
Private property

Rock House
Kitzbühel, Austria
Sold/Private property
Lanz Immobilien
Susanne.lanz@a1.net
www.lanz-residences.com

Haus Hild
Kitzbühel, Austria
Private property

Alpine Mountain Retreat Kitzbühel
Kitzbühel, Austria
Private property

Chalet in Kitzbühel
Kitzbühel, Austria
Sold/Private property
Engel & Völkers Kitzbühel
kitzbuehel@engelvoelkers.com
www.engelvoelkers.com/at/kitzbuehel

Chalet Tauern
Kitzbühel, Austria
Sold/Private property
Lanz Immobilien
Susanne.lanz@a1.net
www.lanz-residences.com

Chalet Sonnenhof
Seefeld, Austria
Sold/Private property
Lanz Immobilien
Susanne.lanz@a1.net
www.lanz-residences.com

Stadl am Tunauberg
South Styria, Austria
For rent as vacation residence
PURESLeben
info@puresleben.at
www.puresleben.at

Amazon Creek
Chamonix, France
For rent as vacation residence
inspire@osprivatetravel.com
www.osprivatetravel.com

Chalet Atlantique
Courchevel, France
For rent as vacation residence
info@chaletatlantique.com
www.chaletatlantique.com
www.earlcrown.com

Ferme de Montagne
Les Gets, France
For rent as vacation residence
enquiries@fermedemontagne.com
www.fermedemontagne.com

Chalet Eco Farm
Les Houches, France
For rent as vacation residence
Huski Alpine Holidays
ski@huski.com
www.huski.com

Le Chalet des Fermes de Marie
Megève, France
For rent as vacation residence
www.chalets.fermesdemarie.com

Le Chalet
Megève, France
For rent as vacation residence
contact@lechaletzannier.com
www.lechaletzannier.com

Chalet Les Brames
Méribel, France
For rent as vacation residence
info@chaletbrames.com
www.chaletbrames.com

Chalet la Transhumance
Saint-Martin-de-Belleville, France
Private property
www.duendepr.com

House in Val d'Isère
Val d'Isère, Switzerland
Private property
Nicky Dobree Interior Design
info@nickydobree.com
www.nickydobree.com

BergLodge
Nesselwang, Germany
For rent as vacation residence
info@berglodge.de
www.berglodge.de

San Lorenzo Mountain Lodge
St. Lorenzen, Italy
For rent as vacation residence
info@sanlorenzomountainlodge.it
www.sanlorenzomountainlodge.it

Mountain Lodge Trysil
Trøgstad, Norway
For rent as vacation residence
post@ mountainlodgetrysil.no
www.mountainlodgetrysil.no
www.christiansoghennie.no

The Villa at Copperhill Mountain Lodge
Åre, Sweden
For rent as vacation residence
info@copperhill.se
www.copperhill.se

Chalet Rougemont
Gstaad Valley, Switzerland
Private property
Tamara's Design
info@tamarasdesign
www.tamarasdesign.com

Chesa Farrer
Celerina, Switzerland
Private property

Julierhof
Champfèr, Switzerland
Private property

Chesa Alta
La Punt, Switzerland
Private property

House in Les Collons
Les Collons, Switzerland
Private property
Nicky Dobree Interior Design
info@nickydobree.com
www.nickydobree.com

Chesa Cresta
St. Moritz, Switzerland
Private property

Chesa Musi
St. Moritz, Switzerland
Private property

Chesa Nova
St. Moritz, Switzerland
Private property

Chesa Pichalain
St. Moritz, Switzerland
Private property

Der Turm
St. Moritz, Switzerland
Private property

La Quinta
St. Moritz, Switzerland
Private property

Olympiastadion
St. Moritz, Switzerland
Private property

Residenzia Rosatsch
St. Moritz, Switzerland
Private property

La Stailina
Suvretta, Switzerland
Private property

Hidden Dragon
Valais, Switzerland
Rooms for rent as vacation home
frontdesk@hidden-dragon.com
www.hidden-dragon.com

Chalet in Verbier
Verbier, Switzerland
Private property
Tamara's Design
info@tamarasdesign
www.tamarasdesign.com

The Lodge
Verbier, Switzerland
For rent as vacation residence
enquiries@virginlimitededition.com
www.thelodge.virgin.com

Zermatt Peak
Zermatt, Switzerland
For rent as vacation residence
The Oxford Ski Company
info@oxfordski.com
www.oxfordski.com

Belmont
Whistler, British Columbia, Canada
Private property
The Luxury Chalet Collection
sales@luxurychaletcollection.com
www.luxurychaletcollection.com

Bighorn
Revelstoke, Canada
For rent as vacation residence
Consensio Holidays
enquiries@consensioholidays.co.uk
www.consensioholidays.co.uk

Pioneer Springs
Aspen, Colorado, USA
For rent as vacation residence
The Oxford Ski Company
info@oxfordski.com
www.oxfordski.com

Chalet Antonia
Aspen, Colorado, USA
For rent as vacation residence
The Oxford Ski Company
info@oxfordski.com
www.oxfordski.com

Mountain Star Residence
Avon, Colorado, USA
Private property
Berglund Architects
www.berglundarchitects.com

Rosenbach Residence
Vail, Colorado, USA
Private property
K.H. Webb Architects
www.khwebb.com

Urban Chalet
Park City, Utah, USA
Private property
www.urban-chalet.com

Miyabi and Tsubaki
Niseko, Japan
For rent as vacation residences
Zekkei Properties
www.zekkei-properties.com

Zekkei
Hirafu, Japan
For rent as vacation residence
Zekkei Properties
www.zekkei-properties.com

House at the Mountain
Karuizawa, Japan
Private property
Miurashin Architect + Associates
www.miurashin.com

Whare Kea Lodge & Chalet
Wanaka, New Zealand
Rooms for rent as vacation home
admin@wharekealodge.com
www.wharekealodge.com

Credits & Imprint

Cover photo by Frédéric Ducout

Back cover photo by Philip Vile, design by Nicky Dobree

pp. 02–03 (Contents) courtesy of Tamara's Design, Günter Standl/www.guenterstandl.de, Roland F. Bauer, Alex Hana & Leo Trippi, Roland F. Bauer, courtesy of Virgin Limited Edition

pp. 04–09 (Introduction)
p. 05 (Amazon Creek) by Sarel Jansen;
p. 06 (San Lorenzo Mountain Lodge) by Annette Fischer/www.annettefischer.ch;
p. 09 (Chalet Atlantique) by Gérard Cottet

pp. 10–13 (Bärenhütte) by David Burghardt

pp. 14–19 (Rock House) by Quirin Leppert/Lanz GmbH

pp. 20–23 (Haus Hild) courtesy of Hild Home Design GmbH

pp. 24–27 (Alpine Mountain Retreat Kitzbühel) by David Burghardt

pp. 28–31 (Chalet in Kitzbühel) by David Burghardt

pp. 32–35 (Chalet Tauern) by Quirin Leppert/Lanz GmbH

pp. 36–39 (Chalet Sonnenhof) by Quirin Leppert/Lanz GmbH

pp. 40–43 (Stadl am Tunauberg) by Günter Standl/www.guenterstandl.de

pp. 44–47 (Amazon Creek) by Sarel Jansen

pp. 48–53 (Chalet Atlantique) by Gérard Cottet

pp. 54–57 (Ferme de Montagne) by Renée Del Missier

pp. 58–61 (Chalet Eco Farm) by Rob Lea/courtesy of Huski Alpine Holiday

pp. 62–65 (Le Chalet des Fermes de Marie)
p. 62, 64, and 65 bottom by L. Di Orio/courtesy of Les Chalets des Fermes;
p. 63 and 65 top (2) by Frédéric Ducout

pp. 66–69 (Le Chalet) courtesy of Chalet Zannier

pp. 70–73 (Chalet Les Brames) by Ross Woodhall

pp. 74–77 (Chalet la Transhumance) by Vincent Leroux

pp. 78–81 (House in Val d'Isère) by Philip Vile, design by Nicky Dobree

pp. 82–85 (BergLodge) by Günter Standl/www.guenterstandl.de

pp. 86–89 (San Lorenzo Mountain Lodge) by Annette Fischer/www.annettefischer.ch

pp. 90–93 (Mountain Lodge Trysil) courtesy of Christian's & Hennie

pp. 94–97 (The Villa at Copperhill Mountain Lodge) by Gösta Fries Photography

pp. 98–101 (Chalet Rougemont) courtesy of Tamara's Design

pp. 102–105 (Chesa Farrer) by Roland F. Bauer

pp. 106–109 (Julierhof) by Roland F. Bauer

pp. 110–113 (Chesa Alta) by Roland F. Bauer

pp. 114–117 (House in Les Collons) by Philip Vile, design by Nicky Dobree

pp. 118–121 (Chesa Cresta) by Roland F. Bauer

pp. 122–125 (Chesa Musi) by Roland F. Bauer

pp. 126–129 (Chesa Nova) by Roland F. Bauer

pp. 130–133 (Chesa Pichalain) by Roland F. Bauer

pp. 134–137 (Der Turm) by Roland F. Bauer

pp. 138–141 (La Quinta) by Roland F. Bauer

pp. 142–145 (Olympiastadion) by Roland F. Bauer

pp. 146–149 (Residenzia Rosatsch) by Roland F. Bauer

pp. 150–155 (La Stailina) by Roland F. Bauer

pp. 156–159 (Hidden Dragon)
p. 156, 158, and 159 middle by Marc Sanders;
p. 157 left by Jean-Claude Roh;
p. 157 right and 159 top by Alex Hana & Leo Trippi;
p. 159 bottom by Stephane Gripari

pp. 160–163 (Chalet in Verbier) courtesy of Tamara's Design

pp. 164–167 (The Lodge)
pp. 164–165 by www.mattlivey.com/courtesy of Virgin Limited Edition (2);
pp. 166–167 by Yves Garneau 2008/courtesy of Virgin Limited Edition (4)

pp. 168–171 (Zermatt Peak) courtesy of The Oxford Ski Company

pp. 172–175 (Belmont) courtesy of The Oxford Ski Company

pp. 176–179 (Bighorn) courtesy of Bighorn

pp. 180–183 (Pioneer Springs) by Michael Brands/The Oxford Ski Company, Pioneer Springs

pp. 184–187 (Chalet Antonia) by Greg Watts Photography

pp. 188–191 (Mountain Star Residence) by Ric Stovall

pp. 192–195 (Rosenbach Residence)
p. 192 left, 193, and 194 by Emily Minton Redfield;
p. 192 right and 195 by Kimberly Gavin Photography

pp. 196–201 (Urban Chalet) by Dana Hoff

pp. 202–205 (Miyabi and Tsubaki) by Glen Claydon

pp. 206–209 (Zekkei)
p. 206 (2), 208, and 209 bottom by Mitsuo Kotaka;
p. 207 and 209 top by Glen Claydon

pp. 210–213 (House at the Mountain) by DAICI ANO/FWD Inc.

pp. 214–217 (Whare Kea Lodge & Chalet)
p. 214, 215, and 217 (2) by Kieran Scott Photography Ltd.;
p. 216 by Bill Bachman

Editor — Gisela Rich
Texts — Gisela Rich
Peter Steinhauer
Copy Editing — Dr. Simone Bischoff
Haike Falkenberg
Editorial Management — Miriam Bischoff
Creative Direction — Martin Nicholas Kunz
Layout & Prepress — Sophie Franke
Sonja Oehmke
Photo Editing — David Burghardt
Imaging — Tridix, Berlin
Translations — WeSwitch Languages
English — Heather B. Bock
Romina Russo
French — Thomas Vitasse
Pierre Fuentes

Published by teNeues Publishing Group

teNeues Verlag GmbH + Co. KG
Am Selder 37, 47906 Kempen, Germany
Phone: +49 (0)2152 916 0, Fax: +49 (0)2152 916 111
e-mail: books@teneues.de

Press department: Andrea Rehn
Phone: +49 (0)2152 916 202
e-mail: arehn@teneues.de

teNeues Digital Media GmbH
Kohlfurter Straße 41-43, 10999 Berlin, Germany
Phone: +49 (0)30 700 77 65 0

teNeues Publishing Company
7 West 18th Street, New York, NY 10011, USA
Phone: +1 212 627 9090, Fax: +1 212 627 9511

teNeues Publishing UK Ltd.
21 Marlowe Court, Lymer Avenue, London SE19 1LP, UK
Phone: +44 (0)20 8670 7522, Fax: +44 (0)20 8670 7523

teNeues France S.A.R.L.
39, rue des Billets, 18250 Henrichemont, France
Phone: +33 (0)2 4826 9348, Fax: +33 (0)1 7072 3482

www.teneues.com

© 2012 teNeues Verlag GmbH + Co. KG, Kempen

ISBN: 978-3-8327-9623-5
Library of Congress Control Number: 2012941938
Printed in Italy.

Picture and text rights reserved for all countries.

No part of this publication may be reproduced in any manner whatsoever. All rights reserved.

While we strive for utmost precision in every detail, we cannot be held responsible for any inaccuracies, neither for any subsequent loss or damage arising.

Bibliographic information published by the Deutsche Nationalbibliothek.

The Deutsche Nationalbibliothek lists this publication in the Deutsche Nationalbibliografie; detailed bibliographic data are available in the Internet at http://dnb.d-nb.de.